Praise for *How to Become a Saint*

"*How to Become a Saint* does so many things well, but what it does best is provide a reminder that 'being a Christian' is simultaneously an act of humility and audacity, quiet daily practices and grand cosmic drama, and a journey in which we don't save ourselves but rather get out of God's way and let everyday grace transform us and our world. This is a simple and personal book that is anything but simplistic. Newcomers to the faith as well as lifelong followers of The Way will all find encouragement, challenge, and practical guidance herein."

Michael L. Budde, author of *The (Magic) Kingdom of God: Christianity and Global Culture Industries*

"Jack Bernard was the real deal, a radical Christian who walked the talk. His walking drove him onto the mercy of God. *How to Become a Saint* is required reading for those of us who aspire to holiness but have repeatedly tried and failed. Grounding his appeal in the trustworthiness of God, Jack speaks a theology that springs from experience and is filled with practical advice."

Jon Stock, Church of the Servant King, Eugene, Oregon

"The path to holiness is fraught with dangers on either side. Between the anxious pursuit of spiritual attainment and the benign neglect of maturity under the guise of 'grace' lies a middle way of the undivided heart. In this book, Jack Bernard guides us through that way."

Evan B. Howard, author of *Affirming the Touch of God* and *Praying the Scriptures*

"Many books on the spiritual life are written more from intellect than experience. Not this one. I knew Jack Bernard as much through the enduring legend of his reputation in his community as through our conversations. His transparent and intelligent words on how to become a saint have the added weight of Jack's life. He lived the pages of this book."

Mark A. Scandrette, ReIMAGINE!

HOW TO BECOME A
SAINT

HOW TO BECOME A
SAINT

A Beginner's Guide

JACK BERNARD

Brazos Press
Grand Rapids, Michigan

Published by Brazos Press
a division of Baker Publishing Group
P.O. Box 6287, Grand Rapids, MI 49516-6287
www.brazospress.com

Printed in the United States of America

Library of Congress Cataloging-in-Publication Data
Bernard, Jack, 1942–2002
    How to become a saint : a beginner's guide / Jack Bernard.
       p.   cm.
    Includes bibliographical references (p.   ).
    ISBN 10: 1-58743-199-8 (pbk.)
    ISBN 978-1-58743-199-9 (pbk.)
    1. Holiness—Christianity. 2. Christian life. I. Title.
    BT767.B48 2007
    248.4—dc22   2006024057

CONTENTS

ACKNOWLEDGMENTS

There have been many people who helped Jack with his journey toward Christ and sainthood. There were those who turned him to Jesus and scripture, his spiritual director who got him reading about saints, friends he could spark off, kids in his special ed class who demonstrated God's love, and his church and family who helped him with his little crosses, dirty dishes, and the struggle to be perfect.

Edith Bernard

We proclaim him, admonishing and teaching everyone with all wisdom, so that we may present everyone perfect in Christ. To this end I labor, struggling with all his energy, which so powerfully works in me.

Colossians 1:28–29 NIV

PREFACE

The following was taken from the eulogy for the life of Jack Bernard, given December 13, 2002, by Tim Otto. Jack and his wife Edith were two of the original founding members of the small intentional Christian community which was the context in which Jack wrote How to Become a Saint *in 1999. He was diagnosed with cancer in November 2002 and died less than three weeks later at the age of 60.*

Jack Bernard was something like an ace of all trades. For his sixtieth birthday his friends tried to list all of the obsessions he'd had. He was a pilot, a racecar driver, a member of the ski patrol, a rock climber, a cyclist, a wildlife painter, a woodworker, a web designer, and a photographer. It was amazing how quickly Jack could master a skill, and how good he became at whatever he attempted. The only thing he might have been bad at was plumbing, but that may just have been propaganda so that he wouldn't have to do it as much.

When Jack became a Christian, he tried to do his best at that as well. He went to seminary, and became a missionary in Belize. Upon returning to the States, he helped found a Christian community, which eventually was called Church of the Sojourners. Early on, Jack began carving crosses for people to wear around their necks. He was concerned that we understood that following Jesus meant taking up our cross in costly ways.

But acing Christianity was not so easy for Jack. In fact, a serious difficulty kept coming up. Those who loved him called it his black hole. He had a pit of despair that he would often sit on the edge of, and sometimes would tumble into.

Then in October of 1996, Jack had a revelation. Writing about it in his book three years later he described it like this:

> This revelation came precisely at the point of, and in answer to, my despairing of myself. I was on the edge of giving up the faith, not because of disillusionment with God but with myself. I had high aspirations of living a life truly dedicated to God but was continually confronted by evidence that I was not only far from the goal but had not yet started. I would repeatedly set out to be serious about it at last but would quickly stall out due to dark emotions or distraction by worldly trivia. I have not been a great sinner struggling with God. I have been a petty one wrapped up in deceptive images of myself. That is just as bad, and I knew it, but I seemed unable to do anything about it for more than a week or two at a time.

But Jack believed that God is *all love*. So the best possible thing we can do is to give ourselves completely to God's will. And because of God's power, what God asks us to do he will also make possible. Jack's revelation had to do with asking God to make it possible for Jack to give himself completely to God, and relaxing. Jesus had to pull this off, not Jack. Failure was no longer a cause for despair, but an opportunity to remember again that this was something God had to do, not Jack; failure became a reminder to press on with trust and thanksgiving. Jack's revelation had to do with realizing that God's love, and power to transform, applied—*even in his case*.

Many people have told Jack things that they have revealed to no one else. Because Jack had begun facing himself for who he really was, in the light of God's love and grace, people felt free to tell Jack the truth about themselves. Jack would remind us, at the edge of our own dark pits, that the gospel, that God's love and power, applied—even in our case.

During his last year, Jack was obsessed with the Jesus he found in the Gospel of Matthew. Jack had a powerful grasp of the Jesus who is reminding his people that they are in the hands of an all-loving, merciful Father. Knowing that, we can trustingly live lives of mercy and self-giving love. This involves letting go of self-protection and the worldly ways of envy, rivalry, and grasping. And it means letting go of our deepest fear: the fear of death.

How strange that this year was to end with Jack modeling exactly what he had preached. In the face of death, Jack cheerfully declared that he understood his whole life to be a gift; that God, in his infinite love and goodness, had given Jack exactly the family and church that he needed to grow into the man God wanted him to be. In Jack's words, he had had the perfect family, the perfect wife, the perfect church. And thinking of his golden retriever, Luke, he usually went on to say that he had even had the perfect dog as well.

Jack, in his writing and sermons, continually insisted that being holy, being a saint, does not mean living without sin. Rather it means being set apart, it means allowing one's self to be completely taken up by God. This book is an account of how that can happen. Not just in the abstract or to Christians in general, but as Jack would have each one of us say, "in my case."

Introduction

The gospel is the direct invitation to real holiness (sainthood). All truly Christian spiritual insights flow from the good news that we are invited to become God's holy children, members of his own family . . . *saints*.

Many of us feel that we have a fairly good understanding of the gospel but continue to have the nagging feeling that we are falling far short of what we could and should be in response to it. I believe every true Christian has a deep desire for holiness, but there is a wide gap between what we know in our heads and what we know in our stomachs. I am convinced that real holiness is possible for me, and if for me, then for all Christians. I want to help rekindle the latent desire for holiness in the confidence that if anyone really wants it, God will open the power of the gospel to him or her and grant it.

The force behind wanting to write this comes from what I call a personal revelation in October 1996. This revelation came precisely at the point of, and in answer to, my despairing of myself. I was on the edge of giving up the faith, not because of disillusionment with God but with myself. I had high aspirations of living a life truly dedicated to God, but was continually confronted by evidence that I was not only far from the goal but had not yet started. I would repeatedly set out to be serious about it at last but would quickly stall out due to dark emotions or distraction by worldly trivia. I have not been a great sinner struggling with God. I have been a petty one wrapped up in deceptive images of myself. That is just as bad, and I knew it, but I seemed unable to do anything about it for more than a week or two at a time.

The "revelation" was not new information. No angel came and gave me a new and secret truth. The revelation was the gut level realization that the gospel in all its promise was actually true *in my case*. I now have hope, and my hope is not rooted in myself anymore but in Jesus. The "revelation" moved the gospel from metaphysics to news, from the realm of abstraction to tangible reality.

This is not to say that life has ceased to be a struggle at times or that, having discovered the inner meaning of the gospel, I have catapulted to perfect sainthood. But the terms of the struggle have become clear, and I can put all my energy into one direction with the confidence that God is going to bring about in me what the gospel promises. My failures no longer seem like disasters, but like opportunities to reaffirm my faith and continue in the same direction with thanksgiving. When the tempter laughs at me and says "Give it up," I can see his form and laugh back, "No, you are the one who is going to lose!"

I have not attempted to answer the many theological questions that surround holiness and related topics such as faith, prayer, and works. I am not entirely naïve to them, but I have not found attempts at intellectually resolving these issues helpful in the actual pursuit of holiness. I am not writing to solve the various arguments between divergent Christian traditions. Instead, I have tried to articulate a practical and comprehensible way to pursue holiness for those who are serious about becoming holy. God intends all who are in Christ to become holy. He will accept any serious and humble effort on our part and bring us to the goal. *What we often lack is humility to hear the gospel as news that has to do with ourselves.* When we can really hear it, the gospel changes how we see the state and purpose of our lives. The gospel changes the way we see ourselves and the world, or we do not really believe it.

In Part I, I have tried to draw a clear picture of what is involved in becoming holy and how one must proceed to get there. This involves setting aside a lot of issues that usually surround the topic of holiness in order to get at the core of the matter. In Part II, I address some related issues. Even there I give only a minimal theoretical framework in order to focus on the practical matters that require our choices and action. The whole purpose of this book is to *uncomplicate* the questions of holiness and to encourage people, in response to the Spirit who draws them, to do what is essential to moving toward holiness.

PART I

GRACE AND HOLINESS

ONE

THE CALL TO
BECOME A SAINT

"Give unto the LORD the glory due unto his name:
. . . worship the LORD in the beauty of holiness."
1 Chronicles 16:29 KJV

Many of us long to be saints. We learn very early to give up or even to ridicule this longing, but something in us persists in desiring harmony with what is good and right and holy. Even for consciously religious people, the term "saint" is a little daunting or feels somewhat self-inflated, as if it were synonymous with "absolute perfection." So we often avoid the word altogether. The term becomes mundane through its familiarity in place names like San Francisco (Saint Francis) and other ordinary uses that conspire to distance the word "saint" from its meaning: "holy one." Through a long process, the language of holiness has become virtually removed from the self-expectations of many modern Christians. Saints are seen as religious superheroes who are admirable, but are so unlike most of us that imitating them with anything more than vague good intentions is not even considered.

My claim is not only that I can become a saint, but also that anyone who seriously wants to can. Real holiness is not the special calling of a few. It is God's will for all believers.

Protestants commonly recognize that the term "saint" is used in the New Testament to refer to all Christians. Scripture does not use it as a special category of super-Christians. This is a good place to start, but what usually happens with this line of logic is a disaster. The reasoning proceeds that since all Christians are saints, the present spiritual state of "average" Christians defines how much (or how little) holiness is required. In other words, many Protestants avoid the trap of reserving the language of sainthood for a special few but make the mistake of reducing the force of the term to the point where it loses its meaning.

Both of these standard errors (putting sainthood beyond us or reducing it to a meaningless category) have the same practical effect. They result in removing the expectation that all Christians lead lives of true, uncompromising holiness.

God intends that you become a saint. It is not presumption to want to be a saint. Rather, it is presumption *not* to want to be a saint. It is outrageously presumptuous to assume we can live better lives some other way. Not seeking to become a saint is the ultimate arrogance, and has nothing to do with humility.

The apostle Paul asserts that God "chose us in Christ before the foundation of the world to be holy and blameless before him in love" (Eph. 1:4). He expects that Christians, as members of the church, would be built up "until all of us come to the unity of the faith and of the knowledge of the Son of God, to maturity, to the measure of the full stature of Christ" (Eph. 4:13). This is the language of real sainthood—even to the extreme of "the measure of the full stature of Christ"—and it applies to "*all of us*." Sainthood is no special calling for a few, and it is no watered-down level of expectation. All of us going all the way together to the perfection of God made visible in Jesus. No compromise with other conflicting needs. No settling for a smaller piece of the pie.

Protestants commonly understand holiness as having to do with a legal standing before God on the basis of nothing more than faith in Jesus. While this certainly has a scriptural basis, scripture never says it in such a way that Christians are let off the hook for actually becoming holy. Quite the opposite is true. *The standing we have in Jesus is the incentive to become holy in actual practice.*[1] In the Ephesians passages cited above, the imagery of growth is used. We are to be built up in the church through other people until we all come to maturity. This holiness is arrived at through a plainly described process in Ephesians 4:11–16. It is much more than a legal transaction declaring us holy when in fact we are not.

None of this is contradicted by the Catholic practice of canonizing certain people as saints. Though I am not Catholic, I think Catholics are on to something good and important in this practice. They canonize people who are especially good examples of sainthood. By doing this, they are saying that all Christians should look to these people as examples of what holiness looks like. While Jesus led one particular human life as the definitive example of holiness, his spirit has clearly been made manifest in the lives of diverse saints in many different situations. They give us a rich and varied portrait of holiness. When we look first to Jesus and then to the witness of the canonized saints, we see that the standard of faithfulness we are called to is very, very high. Rather than finding this calling off-putting, our hearts should soar with hope—because what God wants from us, he makes possible.

This is the first article of faith toward becoming a saint. *What God wants from you, he makes possible.* This is the way forward—don't settle for reduced expectations. Before we move ahead in our discussion, however, let's stop and make sure we're talking about the same subject. Given the popular misconceptions about holiness, it's probably a good idea to define our terms.

What is holiness?

The term "saint" simply means "one who is holy." "Holy" is a word that is generally categorized as a *moral* term, meaning righteous, pure, incorruptible, and having various important virtues. Put more simply, being holy has come to mean being good in a particular religious connotation.

Actually, the word "holy" means "separated" or "set apart." In a biblical context, it means set apart from common use and dedicated to God alone. For example, the temple in Jerusalem was holy in that it was dedicated to God. When Jesus booted the moneychangers and other people doing business from the temple, he was probably doing it because carrying on commerce in the place that was to be set apart for God was a serious contradiction to the holiness of the temple. The temple area was to be holy, set aside for the use of God as specified by God alone. Using holy space for any other purposes was a defilement. Likewise, for a person to be holy means that they are fully set aside for God and withdrawn from common use.

The move from there to thinking of holiness as having to do with being good is natural if we assume that being good is what God really wants from us. That is what the Pharisees staked their careers on. I want to suggest that God has very little interest in people being good. What God wants from us is our trust. Though I am deliberately asserting this in a provocative way, I am also serious about the statement. This is my claim: *becoming a saint has more to do with learning to trust God than with learning to be good.*

A holy people, not heroic individuals

Before getting too far along with the talk about becoming a saint, it is important to address another common misconception. If you're thinking that God wants to make you a spectacularly admirable individual, you're mistaken. That's not at all what God is up to. He is raising up for himself a *holy people*. The call to become a saint is not simply a call for you to become a holy individual. It is a call to become a part of a people who are becoming holy together. You becoming holy is included in that, but not an isolated part. Ultimately, you become part of God's work of creating a whole tribe or family of people who are saints together for the sake of the whole world. When you set out to become a saint, you are becoming a part of something big.

This has been God's plan from the beginning. In Genesis, we read about God choosing Abraham as the father of a special race of people who later become known as the Jews. Even in the initial call, there is a larger picture. God tells Abraham that he will be blessed and then proceeds to say, "In you all the families of the earth shall be blessed" (Gen. 12:3b). Abraham is chosen for the sake of a nation and the nation for the sake of the world.

The Apostle Paul will later hold Abraham up as the exemplar of righteousness by faith and in so doing make it clear that Abraham's faith had a purpose beyond himself. Abraham is to be the founder not only of the Jewish nation as a people of God but also of a tribe of people whose defining characteristic is not genetic relationship but righteousness through faith (Rom. 4:11–12; 9:6–7). The locus of God's work in forming a special people now becomes the church. Christians are individually members of it, but the overarching purpose is to raise up the whole church to holiness (Eph. 4:11–16).[2] The church in turn becomes God's instrument for offering life and holiness to the whole world by calling everyone to become part of it.

Your reach for sainthood is not ultimately about yourself. It is about the ever-widening circle of God's love for the whole of humanity. God's means of growing you in holiness will not be to have you focus your attention on yourself but on the larger picture of what he is doing. This must start with the church, because *there are no saints outside the church*. Many find it hard to accept this, in large part because the church often seems so unholy. I am sympathetic with that problem. On the other hand, our primary difficulty in acknowledging that the church is the central focus of God's action is that the individual is not the central player. One of the standard stumbling blocks to holiness is setting out to personally save the world while skipping right over the church.

But the church is the soil in which God grows saints. You will not find holiness out on the street and bring it into the church as your special gift. Using the metaphor of the body from Ephesians 4, we are being made parts of a body that grow along with all the other parts of the body into the maturity of holiness. Understanding that holiness is not about *me* as a special individual but about God's work among his people is essential to keeping holiness in perspective. Otherwise, we end up running the race in the wrong direction.

Two

An Undivided Heart

Be ye undivided, therefore, as your Heavenly Father is undivided.

Matthew 5:48 (author's paraphrase)

Sainthood is undividedness toward God

As we consider what it means for a person to be set apart for God, or withdrawn from common use, we might follow the logic of the tabernacle and temple. Holiness in Old Testament times included having an isolated existence separate from the ordinary affairs of the world and particularly separate from anything sinful. The book of Exodus is a treasure trove of images of this kind of holiness. Numerous examples may be found in which Moses is directing God's people in what it means to be set apart for God. From the special utensils that are made expressly for use in the tabernacle, to the special recipe for the anointing oil, to the particular animals that are to be sacrificed on the altar, to the vestments the priests are to wear, to the Levites themselves, who are set apart as priests among the Israelites as a whole, to the Israelites who are set apart amongst the nations of the world, there is no lack of illustrations to be found of this intensely observed "set-apart-ness." A dramatic example may be seen in Second Samuel when the very holy Ark of the Covenant is being rescued by David from the Philistines. As Uzzah is helping to move the ark back to its home with the Israelites; he "reached out his hand to the ark of God and took hold of it, for the oxen shook it." Though this action would seem a natural one, the injunction against anyone but a Levite touching the ark was so severe that "the anger of the LORD was kindled against Uzzah; and God struck him there because he reached out his hand to the ark; and he died there beside the ark of God"(2 Sam. 6:7).

To the modern reader this seems like a rather heartless attitude on God's part toward an otherwise obedient servant who was just trying to do what he could to get the ark home safely. But that is not the issue. The holy God has set the ark before his people as a powerful sign of holiness—it is the holiest object the Israelites have, bearing within it the tablets with the Ten Commandments, an urn full of manna, and Aaron's rod which budded miraculously—and it requires much ceremony and ritual, as well as extreme boundaries and restrictions, to maintain its set-apart status. The fact that someone could die by touching it emphasizes with tremendous effectiveness that God's holiness is serious business.

Dedication to God alone takes a very different turn in the portrait of Jesus in the Gospels. In him, we have the Holy One of Israel entering human existence and immersing himself in human affairs. This is astonishing when we grasp what a serious matter holiness is! It is not just a coincidence that Jesus eats and drinks with sinners—it is exactly the point he was trying to make. Instead of the unholy defiling what is holy, as the ancient Hebrew priestly rules insisted, holiness has come from God with the power to make holy those who were unholy. The Pharisees weren't foolish for thinking this was strange behavior for a man of God. Jesus redefines holiness without making it any less serious. Hebrew scriptures had hinted at this kind of spiritual arithmetic, but it certainly wasn't their emphasis. Tragically, the Pharisees wouldn't let Jesus redefine their notions of holiness even when he was showing them that the power of God was behind what he was doing.

Even though Jesus isn't concerned that he will contaminate himself with sinners, the basic concept of holiness as *set apart for God* is not altered. A basic shift in the understanding of holiness happens here, and yet holiness is not turned inside out. Jesus is going for the heart of the matter. He himself is set aside for the Father's use and never defiles himself by turning from the Father's will to other purposes. He is holy, not because he has come down from heaven, or behaved perfectly morally, but because *as a human being he is in no way divided towards God*. He trusts the Father absolutely; his only purpose is to do his Father's will. He is not divided by holding onto any other agenda—not personal advancement, comfort, or even self-preservation. Avoidance of committing sins is a natural consequence of holiness, but it is not the core. Undivided trust in God and the resulting dedication to his will is the essence of holiness.

We Christians have been accustomed to consider holiness as synonymous with morality and virtue—"being good." Holiness is a different concept altogether. Holiness is not about doing things right, or even about being good. *Holiness is entirely relational*. God calls us into relationship with himself. Holiness, on our part, is nothing more, or less, than a wholehearted *YES* to that relationship.

The dilemma of the human condition

So all we have to do is be undivided toward God. No problem, right? We wish. Human history is a long illustration of the fact that the very nature of the human condition is dividedness. My personal history is one of years of riding the roller coaster of reaching for sainthood and then falling away to the point of despair over my simple inability to keep focused on Jesus. I became enamored with almost anything else. The stumbling block for me has never been the fear of some heroic deed that might be required of me but simple distraction by other things. Often the other things were trivia having no intrinsic power—it's astonishing how the smallest, most peripheral, most absurd things can block something so essential, like holding a penny in front of one's eye can block out the sun. The gap between my intentions and my actions has seemed not only huge but impossible—with no means of making serious progress at it. I have been the embodiment of what T. S. Eliot describes in *The Hollow Men*:

> Between the idea
> And the reality
> Between the motion
> And the act
> Falls the Shadow[1]

This is a description of the human condition with regard to the will for goodness. The Apostle Paul said the same thing:

> I do not understand my own actions. For I do not do what I want, but I do the very thing I hate. . . . So I find it to be a law that when I want to do what is good, evil lies close at hand. For I delight in the law of God in my inmost self, but I see in my members another law at war with the law of my mind, making me captive to the law of sin that dwells in my members. Wretched man that I am! Who will rescue me from this body of death? (Rom. 7:15, 21–24)

But this sense of despair is not the last word. This passage has sometimes been cited as justification for accepting less than sainthood, but that is not how Paul intended it. In his line of reasoning, the condition of dividedness was the human condition outside of Christ, but now there is a new creation and new possibilities. The anguished cry of Romans 7:24, "Wretched man that I am! Who will rescue me from this body of death?" is followed by praise for God's providing the solution in Jesus: "Thanks be to God through Jesus Christ our Lord!" This is a solution that offers not only forgiveness but real and actual righteousness for those who walk according to the Holy Spirit. And walking according to the Holy Spirit is, in Paul's understanding, quite possible.

Holiness is in Jesus

In Romans 5, Paul lays out the foundation of his thinking. He says that the whole human race was "in Adam" from the time of Adam to the time of Christ. Now those who believe in Jesus Christ are no longer in Adam but are "in Christ." Romans 5 is important to understanding how Paul thinks about the whole issue of righteousness and holiness. It is often overlooked because it is so foreign to the modern Western mind; we go on to grab things later in Romans without considering their context.

We can't grasp Paul's thought process here if we don't get hold of the idea of a representative ancestor who functionally includes others. Modern people place the individual at the center of everything. The whole logic of being *in Christ*, which is so central to Christian doctrine, makes no sense if you think exclusively in individual terms. In the modern Western world, one active example of this representative thinking is racism, which is a degenerate sense of group identity. In that system of thought, people participate in a sense of oneness or identity with their own group insofar as it defines them over against some other group. This is a negative example, of course, and the prevalence of such negative uses of representative identity have reinforced the Western idealization of the individual. There is, however, a constructive view of corporate human identity that was not at all odd in Paul's time or even in some parts of the world today. In this view, people easily understand that their individual identities are part of the larger identity and destiny of their family and tribe. The idea that people can stand apart from their family and tribe or nation as autonomous, destiny-choosing individuals is a modern notion.

The way Paul sees the human condition, the whole human race is representatively present in one man, Adam. When Adam sinned, the whole race in effect sinned, even those who were not yet born. That is what Romans 5:12 means: "Therefore, just as sin came into the world through one man, and death came through sin, and so death spread to all because all have sinned . . ." Certainly it is true that everybody after Adam also committed their own sins, but that is not Paul's point here. The point is that we all participated in Adam's sin and have received the consequences of that sin—death. Everyone is "in Adam" and has a share in the consequences of his action.

When we believe in Jesus Christ, according to Paul, we become included in him in a way that overrides our being in Adam. There is a new creation, a new representative ancestor. Now, "in Christ" we have an ancestor who, unlike Adam, was completely faithful to God and has incurred blessing, not condemnation. The faithfulness of Jesus thus brings life to those who are in him just as Adam's unfaithfulness brought death to those who are in him. When we are "in Christ," we are lifted out of what we have come to call the human condition, with its problems, self-contradictions, and hopelessness. We are re-created. Nothing less shocking than this is implied by Paul's juxtaposition of "in Adam" and "in Christ." If we are going to talk about seeking to become holy, we need to talk about it from within this paradigm.

From the cry of despair about the human condition Paul goes on in chapter 8 with:

> So then, with my mind I am a slave to the law of God, but with my flesh I am a slave to the law of sin. There is therefore now no condemnation for those who are in Christ Jesus. For the law of the Spirit of life in Christ Jesus has set you free from the law of sin and of death. For God has done what the law, weakened by the flesh, could not do: by sending his own Son in the likeness of sinful flesh, and to deal with sin, he condemned sin in the flesh, so that the just requirement of the law might be fulfilled in us, who walk not according to the flesh but according to the Spirit. (Rom. 7:25–8:4)

Paul's language sometimes takes a lot of twists and turns that make it hard for us to follow, but it is clear that he presumes real righteousness for himself and other Christians. (To fully understand what Paul is saying in this portion of Romans would require a discussion of what he means by flesh and what he means by law. I think such a discussion would simply be distracting at this point. The crucial point is to see that Paul doesn't take dividedness as the inevitable condition of the Christian.) God's action in Jesus Christ made it "so that the just requirement of the law might be fulfilled in us, who walk not according to the flesh but according to the Spirit." Real righteousness comes about by walking (living) according to or in the power of the Holy Spirit. That is what has changed the picture of human dividedness. The veil has been torn. The Holy Spirit is in and with those who are in Christ for the very purpose of bringing them to real righteousness. We are enabled to live in and for God.

It's not possible to achieve this freedom by any meritorious acts, special willpower, or exceptional virtue. It is open to us by God's grace. The gospel is not some kind of second-chance system whereby God keeps on forgiving you and giving you more chances to get it right. Still less is Paul resigned to Christians continuing on in the mix of sin and failed attempts at righteousness that was so characteristic of the human condition in Adam. God has given us Jesus Christ as, among other things, a new representative ancestor, and has provided a way through to a wholly new way of life for those who are "in Christ."

Believing that God will pull it off

When Jesus promised the Holy Spirit to his disciples, he seemed to be saying that the Spirit's presence with them would have power for them that even his own physical presence did not have. "Nevertheless I tell you the truth: it is to your advantage that I go away, for if I do not go away, the Advocate will not come to you; but if I go, I will send him to you" (John 16:7). In spite of the physical absence of Jesus, or because of it, the followers of Jesus have the Spirit of God in a way that empowers them to live lives fully in accordance with God's will. Dividedness is no longer the inevitable human condition for those in Christ.

If we seek to become saints, we have to allow ourselves to be taken hold of by the Holy Spirit. We need to grasp the enormity of what has been promised in the giving of the Holy Spirit. We who are in Christ are no longer merely human! We have the Spirit of God himself for the very purpose of growing us up together in the church until we become saints. Any attempt to live lives pleasing to God that ignores this stupendous fact is doomed to barrenness. Trying to live as saints without the Holy Spirit would be like jumping out of an airplane and trying to fly by flapping your arms. On the other hand, not trying to become a saint with the Holy Spirit as the effective means would be like refusing to travel to Hawaii because you know you can't swim that far.

There is no need to try to *get* the Holy Spirit. God's Spirit has been given to his people. The focus of faith is *laying hold of what God has actually promised.* He has promised to make us holy. "He chose us in Christ before the foundation of the world to be holy and blameless before him in love" (Eph. 1:4). This is the Spirit's purpose. Pursuing other manifestations of the Spirit's power (such as charismatic gifts) can only be a distraction at best. If he gives such gifts, fine. If he does not, that's fine too. Seek holiness, not "giftedness." From the standpoint of seeking to become holy, we lay hold of the Spirit's power by believing that God is in fact in us to bring about true righteousness among his people, ourselves included. We do not need to cajole him into it. Faith is acting on that assumption.

The story of God delivering the Israelites from the oppression of the Midianites is an interesting example of the dynamic of faith and deliverance (see Judg. 6 and 7). The story begins, as with most of the stories in the book of Judges, with the Israelites having worshiped false gods and consequently having been taken captive by an oppressive neighbor nation. The people of Israel cry out to the Lord, and he proceeds to deliver them through the leadership of a very improbable man named Gideon. When we first meet Gideon, he is a young man threshing wheat inside a wine press so that none of the Midianites will see him and steal his wheat. The angel of the Lord comes and recruits him to lead the revolution against the Midianites. Not only does Gideon come into command of a rather unimpressive army, but the Lord tells him to send most of that army home. Only a band of three hundred men remain. These three hundred are not even chosen for their commando training but for how they drink water out of a stream. God then proceeds to rout the whole Midianite army with these three hundred men wielding not swords but primitive flashlights and trumpets.

Believing that God is going to deliver you and me from the snare of the human condition and make us true saints can't be any harder than it was for the Israelites to believe that God was actually going to defeat the Midianite army with Gideon and his three hundred men. This is the nature of the faith God wants. Gideon and his improbable little group (who looked more like a popular music band than a militia) were no better candidates for becoming a conquering army than you or I are for becoming saints. The Midianite army filled the whole valley. The chances of success were almost nonexistent. But that is the very nature of God's deliverance. He deals exclusively with hopeless cases. On this basis, you and I are good candidates for sainthood. Fierce, warriorlike deeds were not required of Gideon and his men; rather, they needed to *act as though God was going to do what he said he was going to do.* What God wants from us is the same.

The key to righteousness from a human standpoint is faith that lays hold of the deliverance God has promised. God himself, however, brings about the deliverance. Gideon did not defeat the Midianites through cleverness, valor, or determination, but simply by his acting upon the word of God—this is called faith.

As we move back to the context of holiness as *undividedness toward God*, we see that in this human condition of dividedness, we can become undivided on one crucial point. *We can be undivided in the faith that God is going to bring about the righteousness he desires in us.* We can reasonably put all our hope in that because God has acted decisively in that direction in Jesus Christ. We can emotionally put all our hope in that because every other attempt we have made toward holiness has come up short. Those of us who know that we can't make it in the holiness game are the ones who can. Our very hopelessness with ourselves becomes the access to the power of God: "My grace is sufficient for you, for power is made perfect in weakness" (2 Cor. 12:9).

This is the how-to of becoming a saint. 1) Decide you want to become a saint. 2) Face the fact that you can't do it yourself. 3) Trust that God is going to do it in you. 4) Act accordingly. 5) Stick with it.

There is nothing esoteric here, and nothing required that is not available to you.

THREE

HUMILITY

Blessed are the poor in spirit, for theirs is the kingdom of heaven.

Matthew 5:3

Humility is not one among a variety of Christian virtues. It is the state of truthfulness that opens the door to the work of God in us. The door of our souls opens with the key of humility so that God can freely bring in every virtue. Humility is not something we add to ourselves to make ourselves better people. If we are humble, we will ask and receive everything from God, because we, of ourselves, have nothing. "Ask, and it will be given you; search, and you will find; knock, and the door will be opened for you" (Matt. 7:7).

What is humility?

Humility is misunderstood just as holiness is. Fr. Nivard Kinsella defines it as follows: "Humility is nothing more or less than the attitude of the creature in the presence of his Creator, and the way of acting which results from such an attitude."[1] Thus, humility is not so much thinking little of ourselves as it is seeing ourselves rightly as creatures of God. Humility is not some kind of difficult attainment. Rather, the natural order of things brings us to humility if we look at ourselves and the universe through the lens of truth.

Our humility problem stems from the fact that we do not want to face the truth. We are, in fact, frequently and passionately dedicated to just the opposite. We struggle with an inner drive to see ourselves as not only important but as superior, at least in some way, to others around us and to base our sense of value on our superiority. Ernest Becker has argued very convincingly that this is a defining characteristic of humanity.[2] There is a considerable body of evidence showing that, far from suffering from "low self-esteem," the normal human tendency is toward an inflated view of self. People consistently overestimate their abilities, particularly of understanding and insight, in comparison with others. Who considers himself below average with regard to insightfulness? (Of course, a case can be made that what we call low self-esteem and an inflated sense of self are not in fact opposites of each other, but rather flip sides of the same coin—and that their real counterpoint is humility, or a truthful view of oneself in relation to God.)

But even if we really were a cut above the rest of the herd with regard to certain abilities, we are still pitifully small creatures who cannot determine our own destinies. We are finite creatures who cannot add one bit to our own lives. Jesus invites us to abandon ourselves into the hands of a loving God, without pretense (cf. Matt. 6:25–33). To accept this offer is not a virtue but good sense in the light of reality.

The downfall of attempts to become humble is that they are usually driven by the desire to become superior. This is the Catch-22 of the spiritual life. The endeavor to become humble is most often rooted in the subtle lie of our own need to be above average, and is therefore doomed to failure. We are inclined to be proud even in spiritual matters. In fact, we are especially proud in spiritual matters because they seem to offer a way past the limitations of being human. What a beautiful jewel humility would add to the crown of my own deity! The only legitimate reason to think and act humbly is because it is the only way of thinking and acting truthfully. We do not need to *act* as though we are poor and needy. We really *are* poor and needy. We are not gods.

We usually refuse to acknowledge this fact, however. Even those of us with the worst "self-esteem" issues are deeply infected with pride. Pride was the original sin of Adam and Eve in the Garden of Eden. They desired to be "like God, knowing good and evil" (Gen. 3:5). They wanted be able to make autonomous judgments and direct their own lives. They no longer wanted to need God. Every time we choose our own will over God's will, we re-enact that scene in the garden. We want to be as gods, knowing and choosing what is good according to our own understanding. God has given us freedom. We are not robots mechanically following pre-programmed patterns. But we are called to make choices as creatures and not as gods. We overstep our limits as creatures when we conclude that we can find in ourselves the source and direction of right actions. What else are we doing when we ignore God and commit sin?

If you set out to get rid of pride or to develop humility you are going to fall flat on your face. If you are fortunate, you will fail at it in such a way that you can see not only that you have failed, but that you have within yourself no *potential* to do otherwise! The key word here is "potential." The standard trick of pride is to protect oneself from facing reality by always claiming unrealized potential. We say to ourselves, "I could do it if only . . ." Therefore actual failures at spiritual achievement are not accepted as a true reflection of self. Before we can actually live in reality and advance in the spiritual life, we must rid ourselves of the notion that we have potential. We do not. We are spiritually bankrupt. Only deliverance from outside of ourselves will keep us out of the pit.

Dependence on God

The key to humility, and to holiness, is not effort toward the goal of achieving personal virtue. The worst-case scenario is that we would feed our pride by succeeding in the outward form of things we think represent holiness! Humility and holiness are found in facing the extent to which we are helpless and at the same time expecting God to have mercy on us. A portrait of this that has made the matter come alive for me is the life and doctrine of Saint Thérèse of Lisieux.

Thérèse never really did anything noteworthy by ordinary human standards, and especially not by the standards of those she called the "great Saints." She came from a bourgeois French family and followed two of her older sisters into the local Carmelite monastery when she was only fifteen years old. She died of tuberculosis at the age of twenty-four. The intervening nine years were spent doing laundry, sweeping corridors, and struggling to stay awake during prayers. The custom of the time allowed no more than two members of one family to join the same convent chapter, so Thérèse was excluded from full membership and remained in the novitiate her whole life there. She served for four years as the assistant to the mistress of novices but was never officially given the title. Despite the limitation of being no one at all important, Thérèse helped reform the whole church's understanding of holiness.

She did not do well as a Carmelite. Thérèse struggled with the rigorous disciplines of the cloistered life. Though she idealized the disciplines, she simply could not keep them very well. In the process she came across the scripture in which Jesus says, "Let the little children come to me" (Matt. 19:14; Mark 10:14; Luke 18:16). She resolved to remain little. If children had special access to Jesus, she would simply be a child. She would remain totally dependent. And that is exactly what she did. From this she developed what she called the "Little Way" or the "Way of Spiritual Childhood." This did not translate into taking holiness less seriously or oversimplifying the spiritual life, but into the expectation that God would deal with her as a loving Father. She assumed that he would be genuinely pleased even by the little and faltering things she attempted to do for him and that he wanted to give her every truly good thing that she asked him for. Thérèse said, "Sanctity does not consist in this or that practice, it consists in a disposition of the heart that makes us humble and little in God's arms, teaches us our weakness and inspires us with an almost presumptuous trust in his fatherly goodness."[3]

The key to holiness is not in our perfection but in our trusting dependence. The opening to God is not through our righteousness but through his mercy. Thérèse's sister Céline outlived her by many years and struggled, often unsuccessfully, to overcome the many faults that were intrinsic to her personality. She clung to the Little Way of her sister. She put her faults in perspective as follows: "I desire only one thing, and this is that God may have pity on me; and one can be pitied only when one is in a pitiable state."[4] Another insight: "I look upon all my imperfections as treasures, and I summon them to appear at my judgment, for all my faults are my strength. Since I regret them and am sincerely humiliated by them, I think that they will draw God's pity down upon me; and when he has pity, he also has mercy."[5]

Our weaknesses really are our greatest assets—they are not simply our strengths held with a bit of modesty. The extent to which we grasp this as true in our own case is the measure of our humility.

Ordinary life

A standard trap that keeps people from taking the pursuit of holiness seriously is the notion that it requires some extraordinary way of life. For example, when Saint Francis of Assisi publicly makes the move to give himself fully to God, he takes off all his clothes, gives them back to his father—whose money bought them—and rides off into the sunset, so to speak. The real story is a bit more complicated than that, but the simplified version catches the spirit of the popular conception. Sainthood requires an extraordinary break with the world.

The trouble with this conception is twofold. First, it means that most people won't give it serious consideration. Everyone can say, "I have other responsibilities." Second, the concrete, practical moves we need to be making toward giving ourselves fully over to God never command our attention because they seem small and unimportant. Holiness is something we seek after and implement in the midst of ordinary life, not something requiring special status or location. Holiness is as available to a single working parent as to a monk, missionary, or pastor. Conversely, becoming *really* holy does not mean one will become a monk or a missionary or pastor. While there are special callings within the church and people are called to serve God in different ways, there are not callings to greater or lesser standards of holiness. "Holiness," said Mother Teresa of Calcutta on many occasions, "is not the luxury of the few but a simple duty for me and for you. We have been created for that." Holiness is found by living out what has been given to you in such a way that you move from moment to moment and task to task in the presence and care of the good God who is at work in you and whom you seek to obey in thought and action. Washing dishes has as much to do with a life of holiness as does preaching sermons. Learning to be less resentful toward others is as important as spending more time in prayer. Best of all, there's always enough time to practice not being resentful. Nothing heroic or unavailable is required. Humility is.

Within the church

The center of ordinary life for a Christian should be the church, which is our primary way of being grown into saints. One of the important parts of that growth process is putting ourselves in a position where we can discover how we are an integral *part* of what God is doing—but not the center. We can learn to be servants and not masters. We can learn to not have things our own way but to put our energy toward doing things for the sake of others.

One of the chief reasons people give for not wanting to be committed to being part of a church is that they find it too ordinary or mundane. They want spiritual excitement and stimulation that gives them a feeling of transcendence, a *sensation* of holiness, perhaps. Yet if holiness is to be discovered in ordinary life, what better place to find it than in the ongoing life of a church family? Avoiding serious church commitments because they feel too confining or time consuming is opting for the lie of self-importance and self-centeredness—the very things that impede the way to holiness.

Being unnoticed as spiritual exercise

Nivard Kinsella's definition of humility as "the attitude of the creature in the presence of his Creator, and the way of acting which results from such an attitude" leads us to the recognition that we are unimportant and helpless rather than important and capable, or even potentially so. (Being unimportant, please note, has nothing to do with being unloved or unlovable. It has to do with recognizing that your life is not the hub of the universe.) This point of view is very difficult to swallow, and goes directly against the grain of our culture, which is constantly clamoring to sell us something which will reveal or enhance our deep specialness and power, and persuade others of it as well.

As I have become more aware of how much I try to manipulate others' opinions of me so they will affirm for me what a fine and significant person I am, I have realized how deeply I have clung to this lie of personal importance and ability. Perhaps I am uniquely perverse, but I suspect I am just average in this, and that such manipulation is a standard human practice. Jesus was addressing this when he said:

> Beware of practicing your piety before others in order to be seen by them; for then you have no reward from your Father in heaven. So whenever you give alms, do not sound a trumpet before you, as the hypocrites do in the synagogues and in the streets, so that they may be praised by others. Truly I tell you, they have received their reward. But when you give alms, do not let your left hand know what your right hand is doing, so that your alms may be done in secret; and your Father who sees in secret will reward you. And whenever you pray, do not be like the hypocrites; for they love to stand and pray in the synagogues and at the street corners, so that they may be seen by others. Truly I tell you, they have received their reward. But whenever you pray, go into your room and shut the door and pray to your Father who is in secret; and your Father who sees in secret will reward you. (Matt. 6:1–6, author's paraphrase)

We do ourselves a disservice if we think we are immune from Pharisee-like spiritual pride. Look closely for the creative new forms we have invented in our own situations. Jesus thought it necessary to give this warning to his own disciples, none of whom were Pharisees.

You cannot seek holiness and the appearance of holiness at the same time. One cancels out the other, just as you cannot serve God and serve mammon: "You cannot serve two masters. You will love the one and hate the other" (Matt. 6:24). One common temptation is to justify wanting the appearance so as to be a good example for others, or some similar rationalization. This is almost convincing; it makes it sound as though we have God's interests at heart. Scripture even seems to invite us to be a good example for others, but this rationalization is a death trap to the pursuit of holiness. What the scripture admonishes us to do is practice the *reality* of holiness, not the appearance of it. Seeking after the appearance of holiness is the very opposite of holiness itself. Holiness is seeking to please God and letting him deal with the consequences to our reputation. Trying to present an appearance of holiness is almost always just the desire (dressed up in religious clothing) to be superior and important. Jesus warned his disciples about this temptation because it is the most enticing of sins for religious people. Turning away from this temptation is a very practical application of "Take up your cross and follow me."

If we see through this temptation, we are in a position to engage in one of the most important "works" that one can do to come to a position of true humility and be on the way to becoming a saint: *Stop trying to manipulate how people think of you.* Speak and act to please God, and trust him to deal with the way other people evaluate you. This is not to imply that God is going to make everyone think you are wonderful if you just trust him to take care of it. He most likely won't. Your being held in high esteem is probably not relevant to the purposes of God. Lots of people, important ones at that, did not think Jesus was wonderful. Some even thought he had a demon! (See Matt. 12:24; Mark 3:22; Luke 11:15; John 10:20.) Why should you fare any better? The Apostle Paul didn't win all the popularity contests either. Lots of people, both within the church and outside of it, thought he was off base. In the event that anyone should actually think we are wonderful, we need to be clear with ourselves that we have nothing or do nothing good but what we have been given. "Why do you call me good? No one is good but God alone" (Mark 10:18).

As a spiritual exercise, refusing to manipulate how people think of you will produce important fruit because it is acting truthfully—that is, humbly. God is pleased when we do things with him as the sole intended audience. Jesus's words, "But whenever you pray, go into your room and shut the door and pray to your Father who is in secret; and your Father who sees in secret will reward you," has wider application than just formal prayer. Our Father is pleased by this *kind* of thing. What father is not pleased when his children do something just to please him rather than for some ulterior reason?

Another benefit is the discovery of just how difficult it is to do this. Trying to persuade others to accept some cherished image of ourselves is more deeply ingrained in us than the most self-critical among us recognize. We can't simply stop it on command. We are in fact enslaved to it. Our need of God's salvation takes on a deeper and more personal meaning than we had known. We need to be saved from ourselves. Become saints?! We are most unpromising prospects. A miracle is needed—and God has promised one.

ƒOUR

SELF-GIVING LOVE

Let us ask Him to make us true in our love, to make us sacrificial beings, for it seems to me that sacrifice is only love put into action.

Elizabeth of the Trinity[1]

Functional images

Human beings are not primarily motivated by a process of scientific logic. We generally do not study the factual data of matters that are central to our lives and then act in a rational manner. Our lives are run by functional images. We grab onto an attractive image of reality or story about how life is (or ought to be) and it becomes powerful within us. For example, there are parts of the American public who have grabbed onto the image of the United States as the great protector of good and freedom in the world. Other segments of the population have taken hold of the image of the United States as the great oppressor supporting capitalistic big business and U.S. interests at the expense of the poor in other countries. How can there be such a variance of conclusion from presumably intelligent people genuinely trying to assess the facts? I assert that in spite of or in addition to the facts, people interpret their experiences through the *images* they have received from parents, teachers, peers, and other sources. A look at historical facts shows some truth behind both of these images of the United States. I am not suggesting that all the various stories or images are equally truthful. Stories certainly need to be checked against facts and practical results. Great harm is done when they aren't. I am simply trying to illustrate the fact that people's views are not formed simply by objective information. God has not made us like computers. He has made us so we can grasp truth intuitively through stories or images.

The way to being directed by truth instead of falsehood is not in striving for complete objectivity. We live truthful lives only when we choose wisely the images that we let form us. Wise choosing is not simply a matter of data analysis. It is largely a matter of discerning which stories or images lead us in the direction of faith, love, and life versus those that make us wither into fear, hatred, rivalry, and death. "The tree is known by its fruit" (Matt. 12:33).

God is love

The images we hold of God are the most important ones we have. The images of God that have motivated the church most powerfully toward faithfulness are images of God as love. But there are other images of God. The Bible also contains images of God as a God of righteous wrath. People who have been nurtured on images of God as wrathful judge often have a hard time getting hold of the image of God as love. How do these images fit together? I do not know. I do know that images of God as righteously wrathful must be interpreted through the lens of God as love and not the other way around. "God's anger is the heat of his love."[2]

There are those throughout Christian history and tradition who prefer the righteousness (or justice)[3] of God as the frontline image of God that Christians should attend to. This certainly has some short-term benefits and is the appropriate word to a people living willfully in sin. However, when used as the dominant image of God, it does not seem to feed the life of the church over time. Over the long haul, a constant primary emphasis on God's righteousness and judgment against sinners seems to slide downhill into a perverse image of a God who is harsh and demanding and before whom we must scrutinize ourselves and each other constantly. This is not of the Spirit and is death to the life and mission of the church.

This is not to say that we can simply ignore God's righteousness and proceed as though he were an indulgent parent. There are those who have majored on God's love in a way that makes him into a co-dependent, "nice" God who turns forgiveness of sins into "Don't worry about it."

I believe Thérèse of Lisieux had love and righteousness in right perspective when she said:

> Since it is true that God's love is deeper and more comprehensive than his justice (it is written, "God is love," but never, "God is justice"), then it is God's love rather than his justice that calls for our response and service. And, because the problem of sin, if we go to the root of it, is not a problem of justice, punishment and giving each his due but is a problem of love, the fundamental question does not run, "O God, is your justice to remain unsatisfied through the hardness of sinners?" but rather, "O God, is your despised love to remain sealed in your heart?"[4]

We fulfill God's righteousness exactly to the degree that we willingly place ourselves in the hands of the God we know to be "all love."[5] The image of God as *all love* can elicit self-giving from us in a way that the image of judgment cannot, and self-giving love is the only response that actually leads to righteousness.

If the thing that gets your juices going is the pursuit of righteousness or justice, you may want to look at what functional images you have of God. It is fundamentally right to see God as the righteous judge, but it is easily misunderstood and distorted. The Pharisees have become a legendary symbol of this all-too-common trap of pursuing holiness out of a desire to be pure and righteous as they imagine God to be pure and righteous. They start with desire for self-enhancement, but instead of being enhanced into God's image, they become "satans" (literally, accusers). We should expect this, because the righteousness of the Kingdom of God is not about personal perfection and getting things right. It is about self-giving love.

Jesus's interactions with the Pharisees embody exactly this distinction. When the Pharisees saw Jesus's disciples picking off heads of grain to eat because they were hungry on the Sabbath, they complained to Jesus. They claimed that the disciples were breaking the Law. Jesus responded by reminding them how David, the exemplar King of Israel, entered the tabernacle of God and ate the sacred bread with his men. This was clearly not "lawful" for them to do. Jesus left the argument and entered their synagogue. There he encountered a man with a withered hand. The Pharisees, who just wouldn't let go of an argument about righteousness, asked him, "Is it lawful to cure on the Sabbath?" The Sabbath and the law were what mattered to them. Jesus pointed out how if any one of them had only one sheep, and it fell into a pit on the Sabbath, they would pull it out without asking any questions about legal violations. Rather than being critical of the hypocrisy of such an action he affirmed that even *their* instincts knew that "it is lawful to do good on the Sabbath."

Righteousness must never be used against itself. *Righteousness can never put limits on God's mercy or it is not righteousness.* After the argument, Jesus proceeded to heal the man with the withered hand, and the Pharisees went out and conspired to destroy Jesus (Matt. 12:1–14). Such is the inevitable consequence of a thirst for righteousness that comes from the self rather than from the love for God who is all love. Destroying Jesus is the natural consequence of holding an image of God as absolute purity and righteousness without allowing love and mercy to define what righteousness and purity mean.

In the preceding dialogue, Jesus said to the Pharisees who were complaining about the disciples eating grain, "But if you had known what this means, 'I desire mercy and not sacrifice,' you would not have condemned the guiltless." Usually this is understood as an exhortation to mercy over legalistic righteousness, but there is more involved. Jesus goes on to say, "For the Son of Man is lord of the sabbath" (Matt. 12:8). The parallel is with David, God's anointed, redefining the holiness rules in the process of carrying out God's plan. There is no argument of principle that holy bread be devoted to common use whenever anyone is hungry. The point is that Jesus, God's anointed, even more than David, defines the meaning of righteousness. All tensions about the nature of righteousness in relation to mercy come to complete unity in Jesus. *In Jesus, the righteousness of God is defined as sacrificial love.*

This is not an attempt to answer all the obvious "But what about . . . ?" questions. That would require much more of a theological treatise than this is intended to be. I am not concerned about people taking a unilateral focus on love as an excuse to sin, because I am not writing for people who care nothing about righteousness. I am showing people who care about righteousness how they can believe that God is all love without feeling this belief to be in tension with any other legitimate image of God. We can give ourselves without reservation to God who is all "yes" to love, not "yes, but."

If we take infinite love as our primary image of God to guide us in our search for holiness, we are on very solid ground, indeed the only solid ground there is for such a search. This is not to say it will be comfortable ground. "God is love" is not a pious platitude that excuses us from having to do anything difficult. If God gives himself away in love, he will certainly expect his children to be like that too. God's love calls forth from us a response of the same love: self-giving love that expresses itself by getting nailed to a cross. On the other hand, we will never be able to understand God's call for sacrifice on our part unless we understand it as coming from the God who loves us with a love that is far beyond anything we can ask or imagine.

The cross as a paradigm of love

I have yet to mention that the word "love" conjures up many images that are inconsistent with the kind of love we are focusing on. Valentine hearts and flowers or other sentimental symbols of happiness and fulfillment do not even begin to approach the nature of the love of God. The ultimate symbol of God's love is the cross—and not just a pretty gold cross hanging around someone's neck, but a human-sized cross with nails. "For God so loved the world that he gave his only son . . ."

We have an inkling of this profound love. In spite of the abuse of the term in our culture, we know that love really does mean setting aside one's own self-interest in order to serve the good of another. A lot of the wrong thinking about love in our culture comes from the idealized view of romantic love. Mothers, perhaps, give a little bit clearer example of God's kind of love. Mothers often work hard and pour themselves out for very unappreciative children. Why? Because they love them, and because they love them they naturally set the good of the children ahead of their own without constantly assessing the child's worthiness.

The warm, human image of a good mother can give us an intimation of divine love—but it too is only a shadow. When we seek to give ourselves over in love to the God who is all love we are suddenly in way over our heads. To seriously consider the infinitely vast, fruitful, dynamic character of the love of God beside our own weak, tiny grasp of the nature of love should take our breath away. This is where the "raging fire of love" imagery of some mystics can be helpful. We are dealing with something beyond our comprehension, something that we cannot keep at a safe distance and enjoy in small portions for our own personal satisfaction. We cannot set limits to something that is unlimited. We want to set limits. We want to be able to decide again at each step of the way. We want to remain in control of our own destiny. Holiness has to do with giving ourselves without limits to the limitless love of God.

Is this frightening? It probably should be. If it isn't, we likely don't understand the enormity of what we are dealing with. Giving ourselves to God is something way beyond human nature. It does not square with the human survival instinct. But what else would you expect on the only road that leads beyond the human condition?

What God did in Jesus

Living in a culture where Christianity is familiar and ordinary can actually make it more difficult to grasp the enormity of the claims the Church makes about its faith. The most basic claims of the Christian faith are by any sensible standard quite fantastic. The claim that the God of the Universe became truly human, in the full, limiting sense, and allowed himself to be killed in a most agonizing manner for the love of humanity is truly astonishing. The life and death of Jesus is not simply a creative extension of the natural logic of any other human religion. Even the improbable image of a heroic corporate CEO, stepping in front of a bullet to protect the company's janitor, wouldn't come close. Gods don't behave this way. Gods are invulnerable; they demand sacrifice; they do not make sacrifices. So the long history of human understanding of the character of gods attests, and modern reason agrees. The Bible does not.

The seeds of the outrageous Christian claims for the incarnation are to be found in the Hebrew scriptures themselves. In the Book of Judges we see the cycles of Israel's apostasies and repentances, and we see God mercifully raising up people whom he empowers to deliver Israel from their oppressors. We see a particularly powerful statement of God's faithfulness in chapter 10. Israel has yet again gone after other gods and been given into the hands of their oppressors, the Ammonites. Israel cries out to the Lord—which is their usual response to finding themselves oppressed because of their idolatrous practices. This time, however, there is a different twist to the story. God is weary of his people's apostasies and tells them: "Go and cry to the gods whom you have chosen; let them deliver you in the time of your distress." But Israel doesn't give it up; they get rid of their idols and keep crying out. The writer then says of God, ". . . and *he could no longer bear to see Israel suffer*" (Judg. 10:10–16; italics mine). The tender feelings of God toward his people win out even over his sense of justice!

Or again in Hosea, after pronouncing scathing judgment and destruction on Israel, God says,

> How can I give you up, Ephraim?
> How can I hand you over, O Israel?
> How can I make you like Admah?
> How can I treat you like Zeboiim?
> My heart recoils within me;
> my compassion grows warm and tender.
> I will not execute my fierce anger;
> I will not again destroy Ephraim;
> for I am God and no mortal,
> the Holy One in your midst,
> and I will not come in wrath.

> Hosea 11:8–9

Here again we see the tender feelings of God toward his people win out over his sense of justice. God is expressing love as mercy, even in the face of extreme provocation, precisely because he is God and not a man. This kind of tender mercy toward his people is characteristic of God's nature.

This doesn't come as a surprise. In Exodus, when God shows himself to Moses, it is with this statement:

> I will make all my *goodness* pass before you, and will proclaim before
> you the name, "The LORD"; and I will be *gracious* to whom I will be
> *gracious*, and will show *mercy* on whom I will show *mercy*. (Exod.
> 33:19; emphasis added)

The revelation of who God is comes in terms of goodness, graciousness, and mercy. I think of the words *grace* and *mercy* as tenderness words or love words in the Hebrew language. This doesn't
make inevitable the conclusion that God would therefore take his
people's suffering on himself, but that conclusion, which is reached
in the New Testament, is not at all out of character with this Old
Testament image of God.

Jesus the Messiah's coming into the world is announced in Mary's
song as the fulfillment of God's mercy toward his people. "He has
helped his servant Israel, in remembrance of his mercy, according
to the promise he made to our ancestors, to Abraham and to his
descendants forever" (Luke 1:54–55). In the Gospel of John, Jesus
spells out for Nicodemus, a leader of the Jews, the divine logic of
God's mercy, which is really an extension of the mercy seen in the
Hebrew scriptures.

> No one has ascended into heaven except the one who descended from
> heaven, the Son of Man. And just as Moses lifted up the serpent in
> the wilderness, so must the Son of Man be lifted up, that whoever
> believes in him may have eternal life. For God so loved the world
> that he gave his only Son, so that everyone who believes in him may
> not perish but may have eternal life. Indeed, God did not send the
> Son into the world to condemn the world, but in order that the world
> might be saved through him. (John 3:13–17)

The word *mercy* in any language falls short of this. We have here
much more than the picture of a good real estate broker putting
together a financial plan that makes a home affordable to the client
who couldn't otherwise have afforded it. There is no manipulation
of the cost, the rating of merits, or demerits, or a limited-cost forgiving of a debt. This love gives itself fully for the sake of the beloved.
God gets himself nailed to a cross as the fullest expression of his
character, which is love for those who do not deserve it either by
nature or by behavior.

Standard Christian doctrine? Of course. But do we really grasp
it? For years, I have been making small crosses for people to wear

around their necks as symbols of who they belong to. A friend recently asked me to make one and to carve the name "Yahweh" into it. I was surprised by my initial inhibition at doing that. Surely I knew any Jew would be mortally offended by it, but there was more to it than that. Christian Trinitarian theology could point out that Jesus died on the cross but he is not the whole Trinity.[6] Technically that's right, but Yahweh on the cross is really what happened. You can't separate off Jesus as a lesser-cost alternative or you have lost the point of the whole thing. God himself, YHWH himself, loved the world with such a raging fire of love that he held back nothing of himself. The cross represents the love of God and the power of God, all compressed into one, and stands as the *defining symbol of righteousness, holiness, and love.*

What belief in Jesus implicates us in

All this is unspeakably good news, and the story isn't over! The way of salvation opened up to us on the cross is not just heavenly fire insurance for the afterlife. We get a whole lot more than that. In the words of Richard Hays:

> *Jesus' death on a cross is the paradigm of faithfulness to God in this world.* The community expresses and experiences the presence of the kingdom of God by participating in the *"koinonia* [fellowship] of his sufferings" (Phil. 3:10). Jesus' death is consistently interpreted in the New Testament as an act of self-giving love, and the community is consistently called to take up the cross and follow in the way that his death defines.[7]

To believe in Jesus carries with it the implication of joining him. To refuse to join him is to refuse to believe in him. The spirit of the rich young ruler, who turned away because of the cost of following Jesus, takes many forms.[8] To follow him is to join him in his self-giving love. Jesus gave himself, in love, for the Father and those whom the Father loves, even to the extent of death on a cross, and he expects his followers to do it *with* him.

Let's turn to another image of salvation in the New Testament: incorporation into God's family. Family members are expected to do like older brother Jesus does. If Jesus is what God is like, Jesus is what God's other children are to be like. In 1 John this is made explicit and applied to sacrificial love for one's brothers and sisters within the church.

> See what love the Father has given us, that we should be called children of God; and that is what we are. The reason the world does not know us is that it did not know him. Beloved, we are God's children now; what we will be has not yet been revealed. What we do know is this: when he is revealed, we will be like him, for we will see him as he is. And all who have this hope in him purify themselves, just as he is pure. (1 John 3:1–3)

From there he goes on to talk about not sinning and what not sinning means: not hating your brothers or sisters but rather loving them. He then points out: "We know love by this: that he laid down his life for us—and we ought to lay down our lives for one another" (1 John 3:16).

An important shape the attribute of self-giving love takes is love for those to whom we are not naturally drawn. Jesus told his disciples:

> If you love those who love you, what credit is that to you? For even sinners love those who love them. If you do good to those who do good to you, what credit is that to you? For even sinners do the same. . . . But love your enemies, do good, and lend, expecting nothing in return. (Luke 6:32–33, 35)

The best indicator that you are practicing self-giving rather than self-rewarding love is to love people you are not naturally inclined to love, even your enemies. If you are growing in this, you are moving along on the road to holiness. If you still have a list of people you can't stand, you are placing obstacles in the way of the Spirit's work in you.

Unreservedly embracing the image of God as all love and forgetting about any tensions with righteousness is far from "easy believism." In giving yourself fully to God who is all love, you are accepting your own crucifixion. On the way to holiness crosses stand not beside but in the middle of the road, where you can't simply pass them by. Like it or not, there is no other road that actually leads to life.

Little crosses

Self-sacrifice is necessary. Self-sacrifice is not just a thing that is required of some Christians some times. All Christians are called to give themselves in this way. It's not this way because God loves to make it tough on us, either. Self-giving love is the very nature of God, and it is therefore the very nature he must incorporate into us as his children, as we become like him.

For those of us who are serious about wanting to give ourselves fully to God, we need a concrete grasp of how to actually take up our crosses. Most of us don't live in a context where we are likely to be martyred for our faith. Neither are most of us called to give up families and relationships and go and live in the slums of Calcutta and serve the poor like Mother Teresa (though perhaps more of us are called to such lives than are willing to hear such a call . . .). Most of us, most of the time, are not in fact called to anything that looks heroic or even worthy of the extreme language of "suffering" or "crosses." Even so, we are not excluded from growing into the likeness of Christ with regard to self-sacrifice.

Our lives are filled with little crosses, and little crosses often feel big in the moment of submitting to them. They may be as small as allowing someone to "waste" our time due to his or her own negligence—without complaining about it. Little crosses may be as subtle as letting our own achievements or good deeds be attributed to another, or (even harder) being blamed for some error or misdeed of another and letting it pass uncontested. "Trivial!" you say. Not to someone who is concerned with what others think about me! Little crosses call for the same response as bigger crosses: "My life is entirely in the hands of God who loves me without limit."

This may be quite a letdown after a long build-up about self-sacrifice. Or maybe just a relief: "Whew! Crosses aren't necessarily a big deal after all." This is not the conclusion I am advocating. I know many people are required to make big sacrifices and to bear serious suffering in life, but even for them, in the day-to-day, it is the little sacrifices that we refuse to offer to God that can keep us from real growth in his love. "His master said to him, 'Well done, good and faithful servant; you were faithful with a few things, I will put you in charge of many things, enter into the joy of your master'" (Matt. 25:21, author's paraphrase). When we can learn to accept all of the petty slights toward ourselves, all the inconveniences and frustrations, all the tiredness, sickness, disappointment, and fear as offerings of faith and love toward God, we begin to be transformed.

I have never had to learn to forgive anyone for killing my child, but I have been learning not to be resentful toward people leaving their dirty dishes in the sink. I have even learned to wash them without feeling like a martyr. Rather, I am learning to do it for God to whom I owe so much love. If I do the dishes for God, I give it to him freely, so the work is not mine anymore to claim as credit. Since I have given my work away and it is no longer mine I am not elevated above my brother or sister. In fact, the other's chore becomes to me as if he or she in fact did it. This may sound silly, but there is real power in this kind of spiritual arithmetic. It is the Little Way of Saint Thérèse, and the primary way by which I can actually live out the love of God instead being a vine that bears no fruit. By taking the Little Way, I am not refusing bigger crosses. I am saying that I am little and that I will accept the little crosses given to me as opportunities to love and grow in God. I will not pass them up. If God wants me to bear bigger crosses, his love for me will make me able to bear them when he asks me to. I will deal with them when they come, but in the meantime I will receive what he has given me for now.

Letting yourself be loved

What I am reaching for here is not ultimately a call to embrace crosses. It is a call to learn to live in love, a call to live in God and let God live in you. "So we have known and believe the love that God has for us. God is love, and those who abide in love abide in God, and God abides in them" (1 John 4:16). I've just been trying to be clear on what kind of a loving God we are dealing with because there is so much false sentimentality around the love of God. Real love takes real faith. But real love is real, and that makes it immeasurably better than the sentimental illusion.

The key element in beginning to learn to embody the love of God is not heroic faith and determination. It has to do with whether or not we can take hold of the love of God as a power that includes us within it. I am talking not about getting what I want, but about losing myself in God, who is more than I could ever ask or imagine.

The difference is between seeing life from the inside of God versus seeing it from within my own sensibilities and capacities. From the inside of God, the overwhelming desire is in remaining there and wanting everybody else to be there. "All shall be well, and all shall be well, and all manner of things shall be well,"[9] because the goodness of God is everywhere and fills everything. If you see life from outside of the love of God, however, you are always in a precarious place, trying to control, protest, manage, promote, etc. From that vantage point, to give oneself without limits to one who is unlimited is terrifying. From inside, it is joy and peace. The Apostle Paul speaks of this view when he says:

> I pray that you may have the power to comprehend, with all the saints, what is the breadth and length and height and depth, and to know the love of Christ that surpasses knowledge, so that you may be filled with all the fullness of God. Now to him who by the power at work within us is able to accomplish abundantly far more than all we can ask or imagine, to him be glory in the church and in Christ Jesus to all generations, forever and ever. Amen. (Eph. 3:18–21)

From that standpoint he is able to say to the Philippian church when they are suffering:

> For he has graciously granted you the privilege not only of believing in Christ, but of suffering for him as well—since you are having the same struggle that you saw I had and now hear that I still have. (Phil. 1:29–30)

From inside the love of God, suffering becomes not only bearable, but a privilege of participating with Christ in his love for the world. This cannot be rationally explained or justified, but it is the fruit of a life trustingly lived in and for God who is all love. It is the wellspring of sainthood.

hundred years old), or when he considered the barrenness of Sarah's womb. No distrust made him waver concerning the promise of God, but he grew strong in his faith as he gave glory to God, being fully convinced that God was able to do what he had promised. Therefore his faith "was reckoned to him as righteousness." (Rom. 4:18–22)

Abraham's faith, held up as the example for all believers, was confidence that God would do what he had promised, in spite of the fact that it was impossible.

We are not to decide what we want and then try to enlist God's support by our faith. We can't go through the scriptures as if they were a catalog, looking for things we can interpret as promises for ourselves and then order them. I remember once hearing a well known "name it and claim it" preacher tell of his wife's desire for a swimming pool. She claimed it by faith on the basis of "May he give you the desire of your heart," and sure enough she got her swimming pool.[1] Granted, this is a somewhat extreme example of the misuse of faith, but this same error can show up in much subtler forms whenever we link the power of our faith with the outcomes we want to see. For example, if a woman has an alcoholic husband for whom she prays diligently, the measure of her faith is not whether her husband is freed from alcoholism or not, but whether she continues to rest in God's goodness, love, mercy, and power even when the outward signs do not reveal healing. "Faith is the assurance of things hoped for, the conviction of things not seen" (Heb. 11:1). In the Bible, we see that God has given his people his Spirit to enable them to do his will. Being enabled to do God's will is quite different from getting him to do our will. In the long run, of course, doing his will is better for us than calling the shots ourselves.

When the topic of faith comes up, we easily get distracted from the central matter of how we are to give ourselves fully over to God. We have lots of questions we want answered. What if the things we want from God seem to be consistent with the nature of what God wants and yet we don't get them? What about healing? What about evil in the world? Is the problem our lack of faith, or is God saying no? While I acknowledge these questions are legitimate, and often asked in great pain, we do not have to answer them in order to become saints. In fact, the determination to go forward without knowing the answers is a part of what makes us saints.

Our topic is how one becomes holy to God in actual practice or, as I have restated it, how one becomes a saint. I dismiss the "hard questions" because only those who are pressing on toward sainthood end up understanding and exercising faith in a way that matters. Standing outside any serious intention toward true holiness and thinking about faith as a means of personal power or security is surely the road to spiritual blindness. *Only in the midst of seeking to give ourselves fully to God will we exercise the kind of faith Jesus calls us to.*

Skipping over the complex questions about faith and answered prayer, we can still know we are on solid ground by claiming as our own God's promise to grow us into holiness. Such a claim is not in the spirit of getting from God what we want, but rather giving to God what he wants: our participation in his central purposes. He wants to make us holy. Claiming his promise of holiness is bringing our wills into conformity with his will with full confidence in his love and goodness. As for getting what we want, becoming holy is the best and greatest of all possible blessings that we and those we love could receive from God.

The question of humility

Laying claim to sainthood for oneself may seem arrogant. There are certainly those who adopt a "holier than thou" posture that we all find very unpleasant. Trying to stand above others is, of course, not real holiness or even the hope of real holiness. It is a counterfeit holiness that stakes its claim on its own virtue.

Laying claim to God's promised holiness is not the same as claiming to have arrived at this state. The Apostle Paul is clear on this when he writes: "Not that I have already obtained this or have already reached the goal; but I press on to make it my own, because Christ Jesus has made me his own" (Phil. 3:12).

Saints do not generally consider themselves holy. They are usually unaware of their own holiness relative to others. First of all, they are not looking to compare, but that is not the important part. The more one tries sincerely to give oneself fully to God, the more one is likely to be painfully aware of one's shortcomings. People who are genuinely the most advanced in the spiritual life are, ironically, the ones who see most clearly how sinful and twisted they really are.

This is not a false humility. It is seeing truly. Their response is not despair, however, but faith in the goodness of God to overcome all the obstacles. Paul says, "I press on to make it my own, *because Christ Jesus has made me his own*" (Phil. 3:12b; emphasis added). Pressing on is the only sane response if we grasp what God has done and what he intends for us. The response of faith to seeing your own unworthiness alongside God's goodness is to go forward in hope, not to withdraw in discouragement.

Breaking away from discouragement in the pursuit of holiness is what made Thérèse of Lisieux such a breath of fresh air. She put holiness back within reach of real people through her Little Way. The need for such a break must have been great: the church accepted her Little Way and canonized her as a saint only thirty years after her death! In pointing a way to holiness that was founded solidly on the biblical picture of God as "merciful love," she was not engaging in fanciful wishing. She was taking hold of a biblical picture of God. We can lay claim to holiness because scripture reveals this as a central purpose of God for his people. Our holiness is God's own chosen and revealed purpose. Our laying hold of it is giving ourselves over to his will.

The truly humble response is to expect God's promise to be true in our own case, as well as in the case of others, in spite of all obstacles, our own unworthiness included. Faith is, on the one hand, an act of determined effort on our part to hold on to what God has promised. On the other hand, it is an expression of dependence on God in the light of our own helplessness, which is virtually the definition of humility. As we saw in an earlier chapter, humility is seeing our condition truly and embracing God's revelation of his goodness. The alternative to laying hold of this is not humility, but unbelief or rebellion.

The conviction of things not seen

"Let us not be disheartened, even when the horizon of history grows dim and closes in, as though human realities made impossible the accomplishment of God's plans."[2]

Humble confidence in God, and not a psychological state of certainty, is the key to faith. Until I grasped this, I was always at sea in my search for faith. We trust God on the basis of his love for us as revealed in Jesus. At times, believing that you have an all-powerful loving father who is looking out for you will be very difficult. In those times, faith will be expressed as a determined effort to have confidence that God loves you and is present in your situation for your ultimate good. This applies to all of life's difficulties: family problems, health problems, economic problems, church problems, you name it. Some of the early Christians had to face Roman lions—a situation that could certainly lead believers to conclude that God had abandoned them. Many of those Christians responded with faith. They concluded that God was with them for good even in death. Jesus had said:

> You will be betrayed even by parents and brothers, by relatives and friends; and they will put some of you to death. You will be hated by all because of my name. But not a hair of your head will perish. By your endurance you will gain your souls. (Luke 21:16–19)

Unlike those Christians facing the lions, most of the challenges to our modern, Western faith don't arise because we are Christian. They arise out of the vulnerability of being frail human beings. We often respond to our own frailty with the determination that, as Christians, we should rise above such weakness. Yet our Father has chosen to leave us in the world, vulnerable to trials and suffering that go with being human. Where we can rise above the human condition is in facing these trials with the faith that God is in them for good. "Now faith is the assurance of things hoped for, the conviction of things not seen" (Heb. 11:1). We are not necessarily delivered from suffering. *When trials are faced with faith we are transformed in the midst of suffering.* God intends that difficulties happen to us that challenge our faith. This is not because he is uncaring and doesn't know the cost. He wants us to face hardships because it is the only means by which we can acquire the character of his true children. Faith is able to hold firmly to confidence in God's goodness and grow through every difficulty encountered.

The conviction of things not felt

One of the natural temptations many of us face is to think of faith as a feeling. Imagining that my faith goes up or down with my feelings of the day will be a serious obstacle to spiritual growth. The equation of faith and feelings might easily lead to the conclusion that an antidepressant is the key to growth in faith. While most people know that is not true, it is the logical extension of confusing faith with feelings. For example, it seems almost impossible for a person to feel depressed and believe that God loves him or her. The other side of this misunderstanding is that, in an effort to persuade ourselves that we have faith, we try to manipulate our feelings in the direction of feeling "up." If we succeed, we may think it is God affirming whatever we are doing. If the effort to feel "up" doesn't work, we may believe God has abandoned us. *Faith is the practical adherence to the trustworthiness of God.* In the long run, faith has an effect on feelings, but there is no one-to-one correlation between faith and feelings, especially in the moment. The presence of good feelings about God does not prove I'm doing well spiritually, and the absence of such feelings doesn't prove I'm not. Thinking and acting as though I have real confidence in the trustworthiness of God is what he wants from me and what opens the door for him to transform me into his likeness. The same response of faith, in relation to any kind of difficulty or challenge, applies equally to difficult feelings.

In all that I am saying on this topic, I am assuming that you are sincerely intending to do God's will and not cling to your own. Negative emotions can be a sign that you are clinging to your own willfulness. Feelings of anger are particularly suspect in this regard. As you face into negative emotions, consider whether there is something behind them that requires simple repentance as a first response before moving on to the line of reasoning that follows.

It takes more faith to act as though you have confidence in the goodness of God when you have no warm assuring feelings than it does when such feelings are present. When you are immersed in the chilly sensation of God's absence, it takes faith to stick with the conviction that you are loved by God and that he is entirely trustworthy in your particular case. There is a substantial body of Christian tradition that insists that, for this very reason, periods of feeling abandoned by God and emptied of assuring feelings of God's presence are necessary to attain full spiritual maturity.[3] From this perspective, dark and cold emotions on spiritual matters may be a God-given opportunity to live by pure faith. God wants us to be able to live by utter confidence in him even though we may not feel like it at the time. The all-too-common inner logic of despair, though not usually externally acknowledged this bluntly, goes something like this: "I feel God is absent. Therefore, God has ceased working in me, and my case is hopeless." The logic of faith goes something like this: "I feel God is absent. Since I know he loves me and intends good for me, he must be working in ways I can't feel right now, and he will bring good out of it." From this perspective we could translate the words of Hebrews 11:1 as: "Faith is the conviction of things not felt."

This line of spiritual reasoning has assumed tremendous importance for me because it has given me a way forward in pursuing holiness. In the past I had often gotten stuck in the dark feelings of hopelessness and given up. I have learned through experience that these same cold feelings that used to stop me in my tracks can become a catalyst to holiness if I embrace them in faith. What used to turn me away from God becomes an occasion to leap into the arms of my loving Father.

Many of those who have been recognized as saints have endured emotional suffering of some sort for significant periods and turned these experiences into springboards to even greater faith. For example, at one point in her life, Saint Thérèse felt no joy in anything except in the conviction that her misery placed her closer to Jesus in his suffering. By a simple interpretation of faith as "unfelt joy"[4] she described what sounds like depression. I have it on good authority that unfelt joy is a contradiction in terms—but here it is in Thérèse's own words:

> I have to forget this earth. Here below, everything tires me, everything is a burden to me. I find only one joy, that of suffering for Jesus, but this *unfelt* joy is above every other joy! Life is passing away. Eternity is advancing in great strides. Soon we shall live the very life of Jesus. After having drunk at the fountain of all sorrows, we shall be deified at the very fountain of all joys, all delights. Soon, little sister, with one look, we shall be able to understand what is taking place within the inner depths of our being![5]

I get a sense that she actually finds something we could describe as joy in looking forward to joy in the future, but this is not a joy experienced in the emotions of the moment. She is expressing a determined confidence in what the good God has in store for her.

Suffering in the present is transformed into confidence in God for the future. In another letter a few weeks later she writes:

> Let us suffer in peace! I admit that this word peace seemed a little strong to me, but the other day, when reflecting on it, I found the secret of suffering in peace. The one who says peace is not saying joy, or at least felt joy. To suffer in peace it is enough to will all that he wills.[6]

Since this unfelt joy doesn't feel like an emotion of joy in the present, she describes it in terms of peace. This sounds a lot like what the Apostle Paul calls "the peace of God, which surpasses all understanding" (Phil. 4:7). The key is *to will what God wills*. This is our definition of holiness. *The way through the dark emotions is to seek holiness.* There you will find peace even if you don't experience emotions of joy for a long time. The action required on your part is not the generation of positive feelings but holding on to the determined confidence that God is going to bring about the good in you that he has promised.

Let me give one more example. This one is from Brother Lawrence of the Resurrection, a seventeenth-century monk who is well known today as the author of *The Practice of the Presence of God*. He had been enduring a long period of anxiety about his relationship with God. He writes:

> When I accepted the fact that I might spend my life suffering from these troubles and anxieties, which in no way diminished the trust I had in God and served only to increase my faith, I found myself changed all at once. And my soul, until that time always in turmoil, experienced a deep inner peace.[7]

There is no virtue in simply resigning yourself to bad feelings. Brother Lawrence is saying that he finally *accepted his troubles and anxieties as being within the power and care of God whom he trusted.* This is another example of suffering being transformed by simply willing what God wills. In this, darkness is turned into light.

Trusting God in ordinary life

Ultimately faith is trust in God that directs the way we think and act. Thinking and acting take place in every moment of our lives, so each moment of our lives becomes an opportunity for faith. While that seems obvious, it is often overlooked. It is easy to see selected categories or particularly challenging situations in our lives as requiring faith. You are living by faith when you do everything that you do in the assurance that God is in control of the entire universe—including your life—and that your offering of yourself to him in every little detail is not unnoticed or unvalued.

Six

The Obedience That Comes from Faith

But those who look into the perfect law, the law of liberty, and persevere, being not hearers who forget but doers who act—they will be blessed in their doing.

James 1:25

Act like you believe it

The people who become saints are those who try to act like saints. There is a direct connection between faith and action. If being a saint is undividedness toward God's will, it follows that seriously trying to do God's will is the primary agenda for anyone seeking to become a saint. If you want to become a saint, your part is to remain utterly focused on being obedient to God. "Success" in this regard is not to be measured by quantifiable obedience brownie points, but in persevering in faith. If you lay claim to God's promise that he is going to make you a saint, you will act on it. If you don't act on it, you haven't laid claim to it. You are kidding yourself, and distrusting God.

Obedience is nothing more than acting as though we trust the goodness of God's will in our own situation. Reasons for disobedience always have to do with the assumption that God's will is less to our advantage than our own will. That should be sufficient discussion of the matter, but it isn't. The human mind often makes what is simple seem complicated.

The problem of obedience

Discussion of obedience easily raises our blood pressure. We imagine there is tension between grace and obedience. Some find the call to Christlike obedience intimidating; it seems to put the possibility of holiness completely out of reach. How can there be any grace in that? It is easy from that perspective to make obedience optional in order to be clear about grace.

From the other side we hear strident calls to Christian obedience. Those on this side often suspect people who talk unequivocally about grace. I myself have had both responses. Sometimes I've responded simply to the spirit of the person advocating one point of view or the other. When someone advocates grace without making a call for obedience, I get uncomfortable. On the other hand, when someone demands obedience in the spirit of exactitude, heroism, or a generally critical posture toward others, I find it frightening. All this back-and-forth is actually unnecessary. Grace and obedience are not in tension with each other, since it is the God who is *all love* who calls us to obey him.

At the very foundation of the imagined tension is the question of what we believe God is like, what he requires of us and why. This is why I have argued that the foundation for seriously pursuing holiness is the conviction that God is *all love*. If one starts with the assumption that God is exacting and demanding with little tolerance for human weakness, one can read the Bible and find it full of all kinds of demands that will make life torturous or impossible. However, if one starts with the assumption that God is *all love*, one can still recognize that God requires something of us. What God requires is all for our good, and this means that his requirements are all grace. If we believe that, our obedient acts, even the small ones, become acts of faith and love in response to grace rather than a burden to be borne.

Obedience is participation in the family business

If God is a demanding taskmaster, obedience seems hopeless. In our attempts to please him we can only lose. Tragically, many people who advocate radical obedience imply that God is beyond our ability to please.

I once worked for a soft-drink bottling company, washing reusable bottles. My job was feeding used bottles onto a conveyor belt that led into a giant washer and then into the machines that filled them with soft drinks. I had to keep the belt full, which was not easy. I had to sort out pallets full of old bottles by type, clean out old cigarettes and the like, and then get them on the belt using a tool that would pick up a dozen at a time.

It was a tedious process, and demanding too, because I had to keep up with the machine. If I let the conveyor belt run out of bottles, the whole process had to be stopped, and I was in trouble. The problem was that the faster I went, the faster the supervisor would make the machine run. The only relief for me was when the machine would jam for some other reason than my failure to stack bottles fast enough. I could never actually please the supervisor. I could only anger him by letting the machine run out of bottles. It was a game of break even or lose, but with no possibility of winning.

Many of us imagine that God is like this supervisor, demanding more and more perfection, more and more hard work, more and more sacrifice, and impossible to please. The only options are disappointing or angering him a little or a lot. Then God's will becomes like the conveyor belt I struggled so hard and unsuccessfully to keep full. Unless the machine stopped for some other reason first, it was just a matter of time before I failed. With this image, no wonder serious attempts at obedience seem futile, and the exhortation to obedience produces anxiety. Grace begins to look like the machine breaking down and letting me off the hook, since keeping up isn't even possible.

Over against this image stands the biblical image of God as loving Father. I hesitate to use the bottling machine image, for fear of adding yet another distortion, but it may in some ways be helpful.

Rather than a production-driven supervisor, we have a loving and patient father who wants us, his children, to participate with him in the family business. He wants this, not because he can't do without our labor, but because he wants us to have the joy of working together with him. Yes, there is work to do, but when the belt runs faster than we can, he either slows the machine down or steps up next to us and helps keep it full. He never asks more of us than we are able to do. Rather than being in a fury when we are slow, he rejoices that we are actually doing some of his work with him. He only becomes angry with us if we walk off the job to work for some competitor's business, but it is anger that is "the heat of his love," because what he desires is for us to be together. This is the picture of God revealed in Jesus who says, "Take my yoke upon you, and learn from me; for I am gentle and humble in heart, and you will find rest for your souls. For my yoke is easy, and my burden is light" (Matt. 11:29–30).

Obedience can be difficult

"And not only that, but we also boast in our sufferings, knowing that suffering produces endurance, and endurance produces character, and character produces hope, and hope does not disappoint us"(Rom. 5:3–5). God is not an indulgent father. Parents who do not demand obedience and discipline from their children fail to help their children develop character. God wants his children to have character—*his* character.

"Character" describes the inner strength required to escape slavery to the tyranny of one's own whims. My dictionary defines it as "moral or ethical strength; integrity; fortitude." Character frees us to voluntarily orient our lives by some greater good. In our context, God's will is the greater good. Holiness and character are not synonymous, but holiness always produces character. Character is thus a pretty good measure of the truthfulness of a person's claims to spiritual experience. If such people are not people of character, their religious claims are not believable. Yet it is so helpful to remember that character is the fruit of holiness, otherwise it is terribly easy to fall into trying to be virtuous for its own sake, rather than giving oneself fully to God and allowing him to produce fruit in the fertile soil of our trust in him.

Character is developed only by facing and overcoming difficulty. For this reason, overly indulgent parents greatly hinder the development of their children's character. The word "character" has a meaning that overlaps with the Greek word *dokime*, which the Apostle Paul uses to describe the moral quality of a Christian. The NRSV and many other English translations render the word *dokime* as "character" or "proven character." Within the meaning of *dokime* is the idea of a quality that has been tested by actual experience. When the New Testament uses this word for Christian character, the testing is always that of trials, hardships, or suffering. Christian character is not certified by a cognitive true-or-false exam. It is certified by perseverance in the face of real life difficulty.

If we are persevering, we can know that our faith is real. Proven character is not proof of some kind of moral attainment. It is the proof that we have faith. That is why Paul says that character produces hope. Peter offers similar wisdom:

> In this you rejoice, even if now for a little while you have had to suffer various trials, so that the genuineness of your faith—being more precious than gold that, though perishable, is tested by fire—may be found to result in praise and glory and honor when Jesus Christ is revealed. (1 Pet. 1:6–7)

Persevering in difficulty isn't merely the litmus test of character, however; it actually produces character. "We also boast in our sufferings, knowing that suffering *produces* endurance, and endurance *produces* character"(Rom. 5:3–4; emphasis added). And, in the words of James:

> My brothers and sisters, whenever you face trials of any kind, consider it nothing but joy, because you know that the testing of your faith *produces* endurance; and let endurance *have its full effect*, so that you may be mature and complete, lacking in nothing. (James 1:2–4; emphasis added)

Christian character is produced by enduring difficulties in faith. Obedience to God, our loving Father, is often difficult. God intends that difficulty not because he is harsh, but because it is the means by which we can acquire the character of his true children.

In the section above where I was talking about my experience working for the soft drink company, I didn't quite tell the whole story. I told it from the perspective I had during my first weeks on the job. The difficulty was real: it was a struggle to go to work each day, but I had responsibilities and needed the income, so I kept going. As time passed I got stronger and faster at doing the job, and I began to see that the boss wasn't really so bad. When I got behind, he often came alongside me and helped load bottles on to the conveyor belt. He actually extended far more grace to me than I was able to notice at the time.

The boss was pushing me beyond the capability I had at the time, but not beyond the capability he was counting on me to grow into. I would not have grown into the job if I had not been pushed beyond what I could comfortably do, but in the process of being pushed it was hard for me to see where I was actually being helped. The analogy with being helped into the family business by a loving father doesn't apply across the board, but in this aspect it does apply: *God will push us beyond what we think we can bear in order to get us to what he knows we can become.* We will often find it hard to see his helping hand in the pushing, but it is there, and we will eventually be able to look back and see it.

There are no shortcuts or low-cost development programs, or God would use them. He does not take pleasure in our pain. He simply knows what it takes for us to become what he is making us into—his children who bear his character. As we persevere in the face of difficulty, we are being trained into the likeness of Jesus. We are not doing a "work" in the sense of us having to earn anything, just as Jesus's obedience to the Father was not a "work" in the sense of his having to earn anything. For us, as for Jesus, perseverance in the face of difficulty is the simple obedience of a son or daughter to our Father who is acting in our best interest.

Paul's view of obedience

The Apostle Paul is best known for his insistence that we are saved by faith and not by works. In his letter to the Galatians, he insists that they are making an awful mistake by thinking that, having become Christians by faith, they can go on to Christian perfection by works of the Law (Gal. 3:1–14). Paul is clear that in our search for holiness, we must not think we can get anywhere by what he calls "works." He makes it clear that righteousness is a gift and not something gained by achievement. If you've worked for something, you've earned it, and you receive it as wages, not as a gift (Rom. 4:4). Righteousness as wages and righteousness as a gift are simply incompatible. The only way one arrives at righteousness is to receive it *gratis*.

According to Paul, the old system whereby one kept the law simply didn't work because the law could tell us what righteousness looked like, but it could not give fallen human beings the power to overcome sin and carry out God's righteous requirements. But Jesus Christ has broken the power of sin over those who believe in him and live by his spirit; they *can* make free choices for righteousness (Rom. 8:1–8). Faith and grace are thus set in direct contrast to work, or works of the law, which would earn a person righteous status. But faith and grace are not the antithesis of obedience. *It is in fact grace on God's part, received with faith on our part, which makes obedience possible.* Simple obedience to the will of God is not a "work."

Believing in righteousness by faith does not lead to the conclusion that obedience is unimportant, but many draw that wrong conclusion. Paul himself had to address the misunderstanding, and he did so in very clear terms: "What then are we to say? Should we continue in sin in order that grace may abound? By no means! How can we who died to sin go on living in it?" (Rom. 6:1–2). Ephesians puts it this way:

> For by grace you have been saved through faith, and this is not your own doing; it is the gift of God—not the result of works, so that no one may boast. For we are what he has made us, created in Christ Jesus for good works, which God prepared beforehand to be our way of life. (Eph. 2:8–10)

There it is. Even the nasty word "works" is affirmed. God wants us to do good works, and his grace working in us makes us new and good so that we *can* do them. Good works are not an achievement. They are not a burden. God does not even demand them! He gives them as a gift, part of the gift of recreating us in Christ. This brings obedience away from "we have to" and into "we get to!" Obedience is participation in our family's business, and all the skills and strength needed for the work are provided.

Making obedience actual

It goes without saying, of course, that obedience must be actual. Having a good theory about obeying God is of little value unless we are obedient in actual practice. The next logical step in our discussion of obedience is to start looking at some of the specific aspects of God's will.

A rich young man came and asked Jesus for some specific instructions on God's will, and Jesus refused to give him a list of things to do. Jesus pointed him to the Ten Commandments, which the young man was already keeping, and then told him to give up everything he had and follow him. Setting out rules doesn't help because God's will is not that we keep rules. He wants our hearts to be focused on imitating him. If our hearts are focused on him, he will lead us into doing his will. We don't stumble in our progress toward holiness because of an aspect of God's will we don't know about. We stumble when our hearts are not directed toward God, and we excuse ourselves from doing what we know his will to be.

We can get lost in seeking God's will by trying to discern a specific will of God for ourselves without paying attention to the big picture of what God is doing. God's goal is for us, together, to be a holy people, a people who love one another and thus reflect his character.[1] We see this from one end of the Bible to the other. God's original call to Abraham to father a nation continues in the New Testament as a call for Christians to build up the church. If my life is not directed toward some aspect of building up the church, I need to change my life so that it is! There is no sense sorting out the little details of his specific will for myself until I understand the main thing he is trying to do. The importance of the church is counter-intuitive in our individualistic culture so I can't say this too strongly or too often. The church, not the individual, is the center of what God is doing in the world. God wants a holy people, not just holy individuals. Holiness is a state we grow into with others, not by ourselves.

I remember trying to help my daughter with a portrait she was painting. She wanted me to help her get the lips, the eyes or nose right, but no matter how she changed them they just didn't look right. The problem was that the basic proportions of the face were wrong, so none of the parts could look right. That's how it is with obeying God's will. Start by getting the basic shape right, and then you can work on the details. If the basic shape and proportion of your life is right, the shape and location of the details become much easier to see. Getting the shape right means being a part of the church in a way that leads to practicing self-giving love for your fellow members.

Knowing that God wants us to be a part of the church doesn't take care of all of the particulars of his will, but rather gives a framework in which to place them. Of course there must be details—they just won't be the same everywhere. The particulars will vary from one church congregation to another and from person to person. You need to be a part of the church—and just adhering to some vague concept of universal church doesn't count. Participation in the universal church isn't real unless it is expressed by committed participation in a particular local congregation. And participation means loving service, not just showing up for a prescribed number of meetings each week. Belonging to the church also means making commitments that place limits on your life. Holding on to the freedom to move from church to church at the dictates of your job or personal preferences is holding on to the priority of self-will. A life without vows and commitments that limit your freedom of preferences is inconsistent with learning to live a life of obedience to God.

Jesus directed his life toward committed obedience to the Father. He did not seek his own glory but the glory of the Father (John 8:50; Heb. 5:5). He loved his disciples as an act of loving obedience to his Father. Being a disciple of Jesus, remaining in his love, means a similar devotion to obedience. "If you love me, you will keep my commandments" (John 14:15). Remaining in the love of the Father and the Son is not a reward for good behavior. Obedience is the expression of love, and love is the expression of obedience, in relationship to God.[2] The new command to "love one another as I have loved you" is not an addition to a list of God's commandments (John 15:12; see also 13:34). The commandment to love is the expression of the full will of God concentrated into the life of Jesus and passed on in the church. Although obedience to God's will is going to take different forms for you at different times, you can be sure that it will always require some form of self-giving love in relationship to the church. If you continue to look in this direction for your obedience to God's will, you will stay on the road to holiness.

SEVEN

PERSEVERANCE

He will also strengthen you to the end, so that you may be blameless on the day of our Lord Jesus Christ.

1 Corinthians 1:8

Jesus said to Peter, "Simon, Simon, listen! Satan has demanded to sift all of you like wheat, but I have prayed for you that your own faith may not fail" (Luke 22:31–32a). Almost immediately after this conversation, Peter denied his Lord. Jesus was not surprised—after all, he had predicted Peter's failure in the same breath as he'd predicted success. Is Jesus just accepting the fact that his prayer will not be answered? I doubt it. This was the man who did nothing but what he saw the Father doing. This was the man who prayed and the dead were raised.[1] No, Jesus is not resigned to Peter's failing and thwarting his prayers. Jesus is taking the long-term view of Peter's faith. He also has a long-term view of your faith and mine. He prayed that Peter's faith would not fail. He has prayed that your faith and my faith will not fail. Peter's faith ultimately didn't fail, and yours and mine won't either, if we persevere.

This brings me to another point I want to make about how to become a saint: *stick with it*. Becoming a saint is a marathon, not a hundred-meter sprint. Keep on with it no matter what. Occasional bursts of heroic obedience are not enough. The long haul is what counts. If you fall down, you get up. If you fall down again, you get up again. If you fall down yet again, you get up yet again. (I could fill quite a few pages this way.) As we discussed earlier, what you deem as failures, God wants to use as a means of building character and faith.

My earlier experiences with seeking to become a saint all ended fairly quickly. I would start running the race, but then I would start looking around at the crowd, then trip over something and fall flat on my face. Sometimes I'd just wander off the course and get lost in the forest. After these experiences it would take a long time before I started running again. I would realize I had failed and give up the race. I would try various theological tricks to convince myself that it didn't really matter. What I have now learned is that falling down or getting lost in the woods didn't matter very much. What does matter is getting back in the race once I realize what has happened.

There were two things that kept me from running after failure: 1) I saw the race as a competition against other Christians, and 2) seeing myself as a failure made the whole enterprise seem hopeless. Theologically and logically I knew better on both counts, but someplace deep inside I didn't.

On competing with others

The first of the things that kept me from sticking with it after I failed may not be a major stumbling block for everyone. I may be uniquely perverse in this, but I would guess that some level of competing and comparing becomes a subtle (or not so subtle) obstacle for others as well. Competition in spiritual matters is pretty close to the origins of human sin. It was some version of this that led Cain to kill his brother Abel, when he noticed that his brother's offering was accepted and his own was not (Gen. 4:1–8).

Most of the time when we compare ourselves with others, we're looking for affirmation that we're at least above average in whatever game we're playing. When I feel like I'm losing in a competitive game, my tendency is to give up and find another game I am better at. On the other hand, some people get all fired up when they sense that they are falling behind and try harder. Either way, if the pursuit of holiness becomes a competition, we're off track. In seeking holiness we are not in competition but rather in partnership with others in the church. Remember that holiness belongs to the church much more than it belongs to individuals. But many of us are not naturally inclined to partnership. If we are trying hard at something, we tend to measure ourselves by how others are doing at the same thing. In Romans 8, Paul calls this competitive attitude "the flesh." He tells us we have to decide if we are going to live by the "flesh" or by the "Spirit." In seeking to give our wills fully to God, competing is counterproductive. We are all in it together: if you are more advanced than I am, you will help pull me closer to the goal. There are no grounds for competition, which is perfectly obvious—unless we are "in the flesh." When comparative feelings come up, we can know that we are losing sight of the road, and need to stop and clear our vision. If we actually think that attaining holiness is some kind of personal achievement that will set us above others, we're lost in the forest. Paul has pointed the way back. "Do nothing from selfish ambition or conceit, but in humility regard others as better than yourselves" (Phil. 2:3).

In addition to the competitive element, there is another fatal flaw with comparisons, even if they were actually humble ones intended for self-evaluation and correction. The Declaration of Independence is just wrong when it says, "All men [women too] are created equal." We are not all playing with the same deck when it comes to the things that give the appearance of holiness. We have different situations, trials, and temptations to deal with, and different chemistries in our brains. Some of these differences are obvious and some are not. To the degree that we remember that holiness has to do with being undivided toward God, not with some external scale of achievement or a particular personality profile, we will know that outward appearances aren't a reliable indicator of holiness in others. "The LORD does not see as mortals see; they look on the outward appearance, but the LORD looks on the heart" (1 Sam. 16:7). If, for example, a person is severely depressed, getting up in the morning may be a significant, determined act of doing God's will. For another person, getting up may be just a way of avoiding the headache they would have if they slept any longer. Both people are getting up, but it means very different things for each with regard to holiness. Don't bother making comparisons with others. The crucial part of the evaluation is beyond your perception.

I encourage you to give up competing and comparing yourself with others entirely! Renew your mind with anti-competitive biblical images: body, family, tribe, belonging, being set free. If you stumble, "lift your drooping hands and strengthen your weak knees, and make straight paths for your feet, so that what is lame may not be put out of joint, but rather be healed" (Heb. 12:12–13) and remind yourself that none of God's promises or intentions toward you have changed since you first set out on the way.

Becoming hopeless

The most devastating part of repeatedly falling on my face or finding myself seriously off course is that it makes the whole enterprise seem hopeless. I begin to say to myself, "I'm just not getting anywhere at this. I'm a hopeless case." Repeated failure to perform makes seeking holiness seem like rolling a heavy stone uphill. The moment I relax a little it rolls back to the bottom—and flattens me in the process.

(I'm talking about actual, acknowledged failure. Often people confuse actual failure with being judged a failure. The two are quite different. If I become hopeless when others judge me a failure, I need to take it as a warning that I am off course and running in the wrong direction . . . and remind myself of what is true in the section above about competing and comparing.)

Actual and acknowledged failure is a great gift. Even though it feels bad, it is the only platform from which to move ahead in our quest to become saints. Acknowledged failure can bring us to humility. Despair is ceasing to trust in God. Worse yet, cleaning up outward appearances to cover up failure confuses the whole enterprise, as it is a lack of faith masquerading as faith.

Following the revelation that my hope is in Jesus and not in myself, I began insisting that I wasn't going to get any better. I wasn't glibly saying I wouldn't try, and I certainly wasn't saying that I'll just do what I want. I was acknowledging that I had absolutely nothing within my experience that was grounds for expecting any improvement. If people wanted to think I was a failure, I wouldn't argue. They were right. That realization was humility on my part—simply being truthful. Since then I have tried to talk about these things with a bit more theological precision in order to acknowledge that God's work in me was, is, and will be transformative.

God doesn't remove from us the tension of having our own free will, and with it the instinct for self. Thus we must continually and freely make the choice of trusting the goodness of God's will over our own. The sense of "not getting any better" is an expression of the truth that I am not going to pass over into an area where there is no temptation or tension within myself. On the other hand, I can expect an ever-increasing willingness on my part to choose God's will. My simplistic statement of the tension, however, focused something that was important for me to hold onto. I had to give up completely on myself, while at the same time clinging to faith in Jesus, in order to open the door for the Holy Spirit to work in me in a new way. I am not contradicting what I have already said about determined obedience. Determined obedience is participating by faith in what God is doing, not pulling myself together for another go at getting it right. There was a turning point in time when I came to know that the only determined obedience that mattered was the obedience of believing that God's promise of holiness applied even to me, and even when pushed right up against the wall of despair.

This doesn't bypass confession and repentance for the sin or sins you may have committed in the process. Confession and repentance are part of actually *being* a saint, not just something you have to get out of the way in order to get there. When you confess—if it is sincere—and repent, you are preferring God's will to your own. That is the whole point.

Remedial lessons

As we struggle to be undivided toward God, it is helpful to remember that Jesus is our teacher and he perseveres in teaching us. Jesus asked his disciples to serve lunch to five thousand people. They thought this was preposterous. Even if there had been a bread factory around, it would have cost a fortune to come up with enough to feed all those people. Under Jesus's direction, they ended up coming up with not only lunch but a big lunch for all these people, all out of five loaves of bread and a couple of fish. That would have been pretty astonishing even for an accomplished catering service.

There was an obvious lesson in that for the disciples: if Jesus tells you to do something, he will make it possible for you to do it.

We don't learn our lessons the first time around no matter how impressive the lessons are. Neither did the original disciples. After he fed the five thousand, Jesus offered them another opportunity. A short time later he was with a bunch of folks out in the country, and again lunchtime came, and there were no fast food places around. Jesus again told his disciples to serve lunch. This time it was only for four thousand—should have been easier. Surely they would remember their last catering experience and proceed accordingly. Yet their response was, "How can one feed these people with bread here in the desert?" (Mark 8:4). So, Jesus goes through the whole thing again. "How much bread do you have?" Again, Jesus gives directions and everybody gets lunch.

The same lesson twice. That should be enough, especially for a hands-on lesson of that quality. In the next scene, reported in Mark's Gospel, the disciples were on the way home with Jesus in the boat (Mark 8:13–21). Jesus was ready to move from catering lessons to lessons about spiritual discernment. He said to them, "Watch out— beware of the yeast of the Pharisees and the yeast of Herod." The disciples concluded among themselves that he was admonishing them because they had forgotten to bring any bread!

How many lessons does it take for them to understand that Jesus isn't stumped by their lack of bread or anything else? I'm certain Mark intentionally wrote the irony of these three accounts about bread into his Gospel. Irony drives home a lesson for us: how many times does it take *us* to learn simple lessons of faith? Nothing has changed about the kind of people God chooses to be saints. Nothing has changed God's persistence in repeating lessons, either. The content of the lessons will vary according to your situation and need, but God will keep patiently teaching us on the same subject over and over again as long as we need it. Again, the point is not becoming expert in feeding large groups of people, or in cleverly answering tricky spiritual questions, but in receiving with childlike faith what Jesus is offering.

It is hard for us to realize that Jesus is teaching us, because we usually do not experience Jesus standing beside us giving us directions as he did with the original disciples. This is especially true when frustrating or painful things are happening. We can, however, learn more and more to see Jesus teaching and helping us in the midst of life's difficulties. Learning to see Jesus in this way is a necessary expression of faith, which no mystical experience or insight can replace. It's also helpful to remember that the original disciples *did* see Jesus standing there giving them instructions, and they still had to keep getting the same lesson over and over. Humility requires that we not consider ourselves better than they were. If the visible presence of Jesus and the experience of his miraculous powers didn't get them over the hump easily, it probably wouldn't for you or me either. The disciples had to learn to believe that Jesus would enable them to do what he asked them to do. It is the same for us.

Be careful whom you listen to

Perseverance requires being careful which voices you listen to. Jesus saying, "Simon, Simon, listen! Satan has demanded to sift all of you like wheat, but I have prayed for you—" should make us pay attention. "Satan has demanded." What does this mean? Can Satan really demand to test the disciples of Jesus? Apparently Jesus thought so. As unappealing as the idea seems to the modern mind, Jesus thought the human race was caught up in a cosmic battle and that there was a real enemy, Satan. A significant part of Jesus's ministry was casting out demons, and he didn't do it only out of compassion for tormented individuals. These were symbolic acts demonstrating that the kingdom of God set people free from the power of the Evil One. N. T. Wright in *Jesus and the Victory of God*[2] makes a good case that the struggle against Satan was Jesus's central understanding of what his life and ministry were about. The struggle for holiness is perhaps not so much *about you* as it is a struggle *over you*. Satan demands to test your faith. Jesus intercedes for you so that your faith will stand the test.

All three Synoptic Gospels show Jesus beginning his public ministry with a critical victory over Satan's temptation in the desert.

> The struggle was about the nature of Jesus' vocation and ministry. The pull of hunger, the lure of cheap and quick "success," the desire to change the vocation to be the light of the world into the vocation to bring all nations under his powerful rule by other means—all of these would easily combine into the temptation to doubt the nature of

the vocation of which he had been sure at the time of John's baptism. "*If* you are the Son of God . . ."[3]

If Satan challenged Jesus, there is every reason to assume that Satan will challenge your claims to be a candidate for holiness. God has allowed Satan to tempt and challenge us. Satan, the accuser, will likely say to you in one form or another, "If you are going to become a saint, then [fill in the blank with your own greatest temptation to giving up]." Jesus's answer to the "If you are . . . then . . ." challenge was "Do not put the Lord your God to the test." That is a lot more elegant than saying "You're wasting your time. By faith in Jesus, I'm going ahead with this anyway," but that works too.

Predestination

Over against the threat of satanic interference stands the decision God made, from before the foundations of the world, that those who are in Christ will be made holy.

> Blessed be the God and Father of our Lord Jesus Christ, who has blessed us in Christ with every spiritual blessing in the heavenly places, just as he chose us in Christ before the foundation of the world to be holy and blameless before him in love. He destined us for adoption as his children through Jesus Christ, according to the good pleasure of his will, to the praise of his glorious grace that he freely bestowed on us in the Beloved. (Eph. 1:3–6)

The more traditional English translation is "He predestined us."[4] Why does this term seem so intimidating? Because it means that somehow we are locked in? Locked in to what? Those who are in Christ are locked in to "adoption as his children." There's nothing ominous about that. Human logic is famous for extrapolating things way beyond their intended conclusions. Predestination is only sinister when we conclude that, if God predestines some to adoption as his children, he must therefore predestine others to exclusion. This leaves people hanging on the question "What am I predestined to?" It does nothing to help us take our own choices seriously. The Apostle Paul, whose writings are claimed as the basis for most of this speculation, does no such thing. He talks about predestination as a response of praise for what God is doing for those who are in Christ.[5] He intends the idea of predestination to be an encouragement to keep on in faith. He never makes pronouncements about anybody being locked out, and he never even hints that predestination means determined endurance isn't necessary. In fact he teaches explicitly that endurance is necessary (Rom. 5:3–4; 2 Cor. 6:4). We ought not push the ideas of scripture in directions the scripture itself does not go.

One of the consequences of pushing the concepts of scripture where the scripture does not take them is that we ignore what the scripture is actually doing with those concepts. In this case, scripture is giving a guarantee that those who set out in Christ to seek after God and his righteousness will be enabled to reach the goal. Nothing, or no one, can interfere to stop them. Hanging onto God's promise that we will become like Jesus is not in vain. Romans 8 concludes with the same thought:

> For I am convinced that neither death, nor life, nor angels, nor rulers, nor things present, nor things to come, nor powers, nor height, nor depth, nor anything else in all creation, will be able to separate us from the love of God in Christ Jesus our Lord. (Rom. 8:38–39)

Reading this text in its full context, we see that Paul is addressing the challenge that suffering and death present to faith. He is showing that things aren't out of control for believers, no matter what the appearance is, because those who are in Christ will arrive at the goal no matter what the obstacles are.

It is easy to get tangled up in the question of whether or not this means that once a person believes in Jesus they can't ultimately turn back. More ink has been used on this subject than on most other topics of Christian theology. I want to stick with the practical, and that is what I believe the New Testament does too. It never sets out to give a systematic explanation of what part of perseverance is God's and what part of it is ours. As a proper grasp of grace leads to obedience, knowing we are predestined leads to determined effort at faithfulness. You are not on your own with the promise of a reward at the end if only you can gut it out. What Jesus said to his first disciples he still says to you "And remember, I am with you always, to the end of the age" (Matt. 28:20).

PART II

RESOURCES
AND CONTEXTS

Eight

We and God

In teaching his disciples to pray, Jesus told them to say "our Father." No one but he can say "my Father." Everyone else is only entitled, as a member of the community, to use that "we" which Jesus made possible for them . . .

To recognize and accept God's fatherhood always means accepting that we are set in relationship to one another: Man is entitled to call God *father* to the extent that he participates in that "we"—which is the form under which God's love seeks for him.

Joseph Ratzinger[1]

"We" or nothing

Neither you nor I nor anybody else has a direct personal relationship with God apart from the church. Our quest for holiness can only take place, from beginning to end, within the church. God becomes accessible to me insofar as I am a part of the "we" which is called the church. God recognizes and is open to us individually because he has recognized the church as his own. I hope I made this clear in the preceding discussion of holiness, but I am now going to give special focus to it. Up to now, I have pointed out ways that the church is essential for your growth in holiness. Conversely, I have said that your holiness is not for yourself but for the church. Yet there is something much more profound here than practical methods for spiritual growth or church improvement. Our relationship to the church has to do with the nature of God himself and how he is making his love tangibly present in the world.

We do not have a relationship with God outside of Christ, and therefore we do not have a relationship with God outside of the church. Our relationship with God, as individuals, is derived from being a part of a new organism (body) that has been created in Christ. The body of Christ, the church, is more than just an organization of separate, distinct people. We are in Christ, and from that position we participate in the relationship between the Son and the Father. In Christ we are not a collection of individuals, as though Christ were a large auditorium in which we all happen to be sitting. Rather, we have one spirit in common, the spirit of Christ, and together we make up one body, the church. "For in the one Spirit we were all baptized into one body—Jews or Greeks, slaves or free—and we were all made to drink of one Spirit" (1 Cor. 12:13).

We might understand the church best if we think of the church as an organism made of separate cells. The life of the organism is in the whole. The individuals in the church are the cells. Each is a living cell with its own nucleus, protoplasm, and surrounding membrane. Each cell has a life of its own but only within a limited sense. Apart from the rest of the organism, it has no consciousness and cannot live. It is an illusion to think that we have any spiritual consciousness and are able to carry on a relationship with the Spirit apart from the shared life of the whole spiritual organism.

From a biblical standpoint, there is nothing controversial here. I have simply stated in cellular terms what Paul has said in anatomical terms in his description of the church as the body of Christ (1 Cor. 12:12–31; Eph. 4:15–16). Surely we are dealing here with some kind of analogy rather than a literal meaning, but nevertheless the use of the term "body" means something. The body is where the Spirit of Christ lives. Within the visible material realm of the created world the Spirit of Christ is not separable from the body of Christ. The actual physical church is in some real sense the manifestation of Christ. Christ himself is no longer physically present on earth except in the church. But in the church, he is truly and actually present.

That is a difficult statement for modern people to accept because we think of the individual as the essential center of relationship with God. The reason behind what I am saying is even more shocking than the idea of a group identity. *The church is the visible form of God's presence in the world!*

Let's now look through the lens of another biblical image: the dwelling place of God. This perspective supports the same conclusion. Before Christ came into the world, God was never visible as a physical being.[2] Christ came as the visible, physical embodiment of God. Christ is the form that God took when his love moved him to enter his own physical creation. But Christ is no longer visible to us. He returned to the Father who sent his Holy Spirit, but the Spirit is not visible to us or to the world. The Spirit formed and indwells the church,[3] and the church is visible and physically present in the world. The Spirit created the church as God's dwelling place, a temple for God's residence on earth. The church is now the place where people can seek God and find him. The parallel here to the temple of the Lord in the Old Testament is intended. The people of God were to seek his presence in that temple and not in the "high places" that were judged as idolatrous alternatives. To say that the church is the visible expression of God's presence is to say that the church is the new temple—we are not to seek God anywhere else.

I must be careful to note that the church is not God's fullness as Christ is. We cannot say the church is God.[4] On the other hand, nothing in the New Testament indicates that God has made himself visibly present in alternative ways in the present age. The church stands in a unique relationship to God and to the world.

In saying all this, I am running the risk of getting us off track with theological abstractions. But the idea of the church as the expression of God's presence lays an important foundation. What matters is that you grasp that the church and your relationship with the church is not just a peripheral matter in your becoming a saint. We are not the habitation of the Spirit of Christ except as we are a part of the church. *We must learn to think about our relationship with God in terms of "we and God" rather than "me and God."*

I have not been laying this out in order to prove the theological correctness of what I have written about holiness. The idea of "we and God" has enormous practical implications for what it means to become a saint. If sainthood is being undivided toward God's will, and holiness means preferring God's will to our own wills, God's relationship to the church implies that we could express sainthood very concretely as living our lives in and for the church! The church represents God's physical presence in the world. We are physical creatures, so *our unity with God must be expressed in and through the church.*

More than a method

Let's look at why, from God's perspective, this is so important. God's choice to make himself accessible to human beings through his presence in the visible church is not just an arbitrary one. We might think that God could have made himself visibly present in other ways. Surely angels or ad agencies would have made a better impression on the world than the church often has. If he were going to use the church at all, surely he could have done a better job of taking charge of it than he appears to have done. But that kind of logic misses the point of what God is doing in the world. The church is much more than a method for communicating information God wants the world to have, or presenting an attractive appeal so the world will "buy in." The church is actually the logical extension of what God has done in Jesus—taking on human flesh.

God's nature is love. This is the reason he created the universe, revealed himself to his creatures, and then actually became one of us in Jesus. In Jesus, God has taken on visible form and we can see what he is: self-giving love. God is a Trinity: Father, Son, and Holy Spirit. The relationship within the Trinity is love, God's very nature. Love within the Trinity is not visible to us. It is beyond the material world. When Jesus took on human flesh, he made God visible. His love, which moved him to the extreme obedience of the cross, has demonstrated the limitless extent of Trinitarian love. When he called human beings to himself and into a participation in his relationship with the Father, he gave the Trinitarian love between the Father, the Son, and the Holy Spirit a visible form. This love is now manifested in the relationship between visible human beings in the church as they love one another with a love that is beyond human nature. Jesus's intention for the church was that his disciples would love him and each other with the same love that the members of the Trinity have for one another. "As the Father has loved me, so I have loved you; abide in my love. If you keep my commandments, you will abide in my love, just as I have kept my Father's commandments and abide in his love" (John 15:9–10; see also 1 John 3:16). "This is my commandment, that you love one another as I have loved you" (John 15:12). *As the members of the church love one another, God is made visible to the world* (John 17:23). In this way Christ, who did not seek his own glory, is glorified (John 17:10).

If the church did everything else right and did not make the love of God visible, it would have done nothing; it would have failed in the one thing for which it was called into being (1 Cor. 13:1). It is in the church's appropriation of this Trinitarian love, the love of all the members for one another, that the nature of God is made visible in the world. This love is what my seemingly rash statement that the church is the visible form of God's presence in the world implies. No mystical experience can take you deeper in the knowledge of God than knowing and becoming part of God's love. At its best, mystical experience can only help you see God's love more clearly.

Making it actual

The preceding is the spiritual principle concerning God and the church, but God does not deal with us in spiritual principles. He deals with us as a unity of body and spirit. Our spiritual unity with God must be expressed in tangible and physical form in and through the church. Love for God must be expressed as love for brothers and sisters in the church. To become a saint means giving yourself fully to God's will. God's will is that you love your brothers and sisters in the church as Jesus has loved them. That means self-giving love that takes tangible and self-sacrificial form. We must love the actual people within our actual local congregations. Participation in the universal church without committed participation in an actual local congregation is simply a lie. To love Christians in general without loving the actual people God has placed in your life is also a lie. To have pleasant feelings of love for people without in some way laying down your life for them is a lie. We do God's will to the extent that we participate in giving tangible, visible form to God's love. By doing this, and only by doing this, we become saints. It doesn't happen all at once, but this is the ground over which the road to sainthood has been laid.

I realize that what I have been saying about the church implies a quality that seems invisible in the actual, visible church. It doesn't take much imagination to look at any real-world expression of the church and find that it falls far short of the ideals you might have for it. Some expressions of the church are certainly more promising than others, but trying to determine if *your* church is a *real* church is beyond the scope of what I am trying to do here. For the purpose of staying on the road to holiness, what I have said above will be the central issue—provided, of course, that you put it into practice. And, not surprisingly, as people give themselves fully to God and put love into practice, the church becomes what it should be.

"Just live out God's love and God will deal with making the church what he wants it to be"—that still sounds like naïve idealism, but it is close to the heart of what faith means. Jesus's obedience to the point of death was motivated by love, without calculation of effectiveness on his part. His death was real death, not just an inconvenient stopover on the way to heaven. He gave himself up fully to the will of his Father without question or qualification. All questions about effectiveness lay in the hands of his Father. Such is the nature of the love that calls us. We cannot measure love by calculations of effectiveness. Crosses are never reasonable or effective.[5] Giving ourselves to the real church, as it is actually present in the world, will not likely seem reasonable or effective either. What we are called to is to give ourselves over fully to the will of our Father in whose hands alone all questions of effectiveness must remain. Doing the will of our Father must be our only goal, just as it was Jesus's only goal. This is the definition of holiness.

Nine

The Role of Spiritual Disciplines

Sanctity does not consist in this or that practice, it consists in a disposition of the heart that makes us humble and little in God's arms, teaches us our weakness and inspires us with an almost presumptuous trust in his fatherly goodness.

Thérèse of Lisieux[1]

Spiritual disciplines are the particular practices we carry out in order to facilitate strengthening our faith and obedience to God. If you actually intend to run a marathon, as opposed to just wishing you could, you set out a carefully planned training regimen intended to strengthen your body so that it can complete the task. While the analogy with seeking to become holy isn't complete, it is close enough to be of practical value. Holiness is undividedness toward God, and it is not arrived at by our efforts at self-perfection but as a gift of grace. This doesn't mean that we can adopt a passive posture in the process. To do that would simply be a choice to prefer our own laziness to God's will. We must, within the limits of our ability, open ourselves to God. Among the ways in which we can open ourselves to his work in us is to adhere to prescribed spiritual disciplines.

Spiritual discipline helps enable us to do the will of God. It is not enlisting God to do our will. It is not trying to gain access to some kind of supernatural power or develop our spiritual natures or any of the other self-enhancing possibilities. Those things are temptations, not goals.

Whether we feel like it or not

Saint Thérèse is surely right that holiness does not consist in doing our spiritual practices faultlessly. It does not follow, however, that we can do without particular spiritual practices that are carried out with some degree of regularity. Discipline means we exert willpower to do something that is not our natural inclination of the moment. The distinction between *wanting* to do something and *feeling* like doing it is crucial. At 6:00 a.m. I do not *feel* like getting out of bed to pray. I *want* to get out of bed, however; no one is forcing me. I want to do it because it is necessary to accomplish a goal that is more important to me than sleeping longer.

Disciplines are not for the purpose of driving us to do something we ultimately do not want to do. If we really have no heart for the things of God we need to go back to step one and face the choice of whether we want to give ourselves over to God or not. Spiritual disciplines will not help us if we are not willing to do this. Spiritual disciplines are founded on the assumption that we at least *want to want to* live in and for God. Disciplines are devices to help us transcend our feelings of the moment and get on with what we ultimately want to do.

For the most part, spiritual practices are boring, not exciting. The point is to open ourselves to God on his terms, not to entertain ourselves. Spiritual disciplines usually involve setting aside specific times each day to pay attention to God rather than ourselves. If we won't do that, it is ludicrous to think that we will pay attention to God's will in the midst of everything else.

Avoid being super-spiritual

People starting out to do spiritual disciplines usually have high aspirations. It is common for people who acknowledge the need for a disciplined prayer life to start by deciding to spend thirty minutes or an hour a day in formal prayer. This can be a setup for discouragement, and my advice would be to start with something like ten minutes a day, then adding to it as the rhythm of the discipline becomes regular. For most people, starting a form of spiritual exercise such as regular prayer is successful if it moves them from doing nothing to doing a little. A short term of doing heroic sessions of prayer is worth far less than a lifetime practice of doing a little regularly.

Be wary of things that will set you apart from your brothers and sisters. The biggest danger in spiritual disciplines is that you will think you are special by going beyond others—which is disastrous. This is not to say that you should abstain from scripture reading and prayer because you are part of a church where people have ceased to do such things. Just be careful of setting out to be more spiritual than others.

A note about concentration

Most people struggle with concentration in prayer and we think we are uniquely unable to concentrate. If you do very poorly at it you are probably just average—but, as in everything else about seeking after God, comparative ratings are not important. What is actually important is that you not quit. When your mind wanders during prayer, as soon as you notice it, bring it back. When it wanders again, bring it back again, and again, and again.

Difficulty in concentration is no barrier to success. This feels counterintuitive. If I sit down to pray for a ten-minute period and at the end I realize that I have spent eight of those minutes thinking about some work I have to do in my shop, I am inclined to think I have only prayed for two minutes. Who is going to become a saint through two-minute prayer sessions? After all, Saint Francis went on for days. The answer to that question is this: anybody in Christ who is willing to. *Holiness is not something we achieve and it does not consist in special abilities at doing anything, even praying.* As for the mathematics of having only prayed two minutes out of ten, that's great! I've managed to turn my attention to God for two minutes. That is far more than I would have done if I hadn't tried to pray for ten. As for how much of that time our Father, who is all love, spent paying attention—do you want to guess? This isn't to say that my effort doesn't matter, but that it matters as a child's childish effort matters to a loving parent. Such childish effort guarantees success because of the parent's love, not the quality of the child's effort. This kind of thinking enables me to persist in prayer and the hope of pleasing God. I suspect it is the only kind of logic of disciplined prayer that is actually pleasing to God.

Repentance disciplines

Christianity is not a religion of disembodied spirituality. Spiritual growth has direct consequences for how we live among the people of God and in the world. The logical extension of the disciplines of Bible reading and prayer are what I call "repentance disciplines." Repentance disciplines have to do with turning from one's sins, and are closely related to the original meaning of "penance." Unfortunately, the word "penance" can suggest "paying for your sins" rather than turning from them. Our goal is to turn from our sins in order to please to God, not to make payments to God so we can keep them. To repent literally means to turn around or change direction. There are practical ways we can take disciplined turning-around steps. In the chapter on humility, I suggested a spiritual exercise to aid in refusing to manipulate how people see you. We can take conscious, disciplined steps like this to turn away from the things that hold us back in our quest for holiness. Repentance disciplines will be helpful if we find things that are truly expressions of our holding on to our own will instead of giving it to God. Seeking our own glory rather than God's is certainly a central problem for most of us. On the other side of the scale, fasting in the subtle hope of losing ten pounds probably has more to do with wanting people to think well of you than with pleasing God. Look for things that have to do with submission to God and not with outward self-improvement.

Here are some more suggestions:

- Attribute good intentions to people, especially those who are critical of you.
- Don't be resentful, but see your brothers and sisters as gifts of the good God.
- Don't speak to draw attention to yourself.
- Stop complaining.
- Don't defend yourself if blamed wrongly. (This is an advanced exercise for those who want to sleep on beds of nails but whose spouses won't allow one in the bedroom.)

These are harder than you think! I suggest that you pick one of these—or one of your own that fits you best—and really take it seriously, rather than attempting to take them all on at once. When you fail, don't rationalize it away. Confess your sin or failure, then get up and keep going.

The object is only secondarily to help you be a better person through practicing virtues. The most important and most probable effect will be to help you to see how much you need your heavenly Father's intervention if you are to make any progress at all. Having a firm grasp on that is the best possible result of any spiritual discipline.

The discipline of weakness

As we grow in the knowledge of God we find that we do not necessarily grow in the sense of our own wisdom and strength. We come to see clearly how incompetent and weak we are. "God chose what is foolish in the world to shame the wise; God chose what is weak in the world to shame the strong" (1 Cor. 1:27). God told the apostle Paul, "My grace is sufficient for you, for power is made perfect in weakness." To which Paul responded: "So, I will boast all the more gladly of my weaknesses, so that the power of Christ may dwell in me" (2 Cor. 12:9).

This weakness and foolishness manifests itself in various ways. I am only going to deal with one of them: the growing awareness of our own sinfulness, which God uses to counteract our natural tendency to self-deception. As we grow closer to God, rather than gaining a delightful sense of our budding perfection, we see more clearly the depth of our own sinfulness. We see more and more that even our best actions are polluted by selfish interests and self-will. Our view of the world is self-centered, not God-centered. Surprisingly, this growing reality, though humiliating, isn't discouraging. Along with this growing understanding of our own sinfulness we also become increasingly aware of our dependence on Christ and his compassionate presence with us. As we grow in faith, the Spirit is able to show us more of the absurd depth of our selfishness; we will better comprehend the depth of God's love and what he is doing for us. "Now we have received not the spirit of the world, but the Spirit that is from God, so that we may understand the gifts bestowed on us by God" (1 Cor. 2:12).

This is why spiritual growth can never result in self-congratulation. If you are thinking you have arrived at an advanced spiritual state, you are off the road and having hallucinations. Even Paul states: "Not that I have already obtained this or have already reached the goal; but I press on to make it my own, because Christ Jesus has made me his own" (Phil. 3:12). Real spiritual progress can result only in ever-increasing awareness that we have no shred of virtue to hold up as our own achievement. This is not at all the same thing as being down on ourselves—the evidence of spiritual growth is not self-condemnation, but gratitude and adoration of God who has loved us beyond all possibility of measuring, resulting in ever greater determination to move forward in being conformed to the image of his Son.

A corollary to this growing sense of sinfulness is that we cease caring who knows it. I have to admit that I have had a hard time learning this one. Jesus said, "I do not seek my own glory" (John 8:50). Not seeking my own glory is an essential element in giving myself fully to God, and it is even harder than I used to think. Self-glorification crops up everywhere. Simply being truthful about who I am is where I must start giving up on my own glory. When I find myself wanting to hide my sinfulness I know I am drifting off the road. Transparency about sinfulness is one of the disciplines that lights the road to holiness.

TEN

THE ROLE
OF SCRIPTURE

Then [Jesus] began to say to them, "Today this scripture has been fulfilled in your hearing."

Luke 4:21

As we seek to give ourselves over to God, scripture requires a central place in our lives. Scripture has always been central for Christians seeking after God. Even during the apostolic age, when the Spirit was guiding so directly, it seems to have been so. Paul, while in prison, asked his friends to bring his scripture to him. Nearly two millennia later, a close friend of mine was in the hospital recovering from a major surgery and, even though he was too disoriented to think intellectually about what the scriptures were saying, he found that having the Psalms read to him was one of his few sources of comfort. For serious Christians the scriptures are much more than a source of information about God and the history of his people. *The scriptures are the place where one seeks to encounter God.*

The presence of God in Israel

For Christians and Jews, experiencing the presence of God has always been a pressing issue, because the presence of God is something invisible and intangible. Since human beings are not able to live in complete abstraction, we need concrete expressions of invisible realities in order to keep them central to our lives. Notions that are simple abstractions without visible expressions will simply disappear from the way we think and live. Conversely, if an invisible reality is important to people, they will find ways of giving it visible expression. If married people love one another, they will find ways of giving their love outward expression. In the absence of outward expression they have trouble loving or believing they are loved.

Jews found an outward expression of God's presence with them in the temple. From the time Solomon finished building it (ca. 952 BC),[1] the temple of the Lord in Jerusalem served as the locus of God's presence with his people. This understanding was not a literal-minded belief that God lived in this building and was absent elsewhere.[2] For ancient Israel the temple was the concrete expression of God's invisible presence with his people. People who longed to be with God found some concrete satisfaction for this longing in the temple. The psalmist puts it beautifully: "One thing I asked of the LORD, that will I seek after: to live in the house of the LORD all the days of my life, to behold the beauty of the LORD, and to inquire in his temple" (Ps. 27:4). When there is no temple, or the people no longer see it as an expression of God's presence, there is a crisis. Nebuchadnezzar of Babylon destroyed the Jerusalem temple in 587 or 586 BC, and took most of the people away to captivity in Babylon. This produced an unimaginable crisis of faith. However, Israel's faith persevered. Their hope was kept alive by prophets who had presided over the tragedy (particularly Jeremiah and Ezekiel) and had already provided an explanation and a hope in advance.[3]

Cyrus of Persia then overthrew Babylon in 538 BC. Soon after he assumed control, the Jews were again allowed to return to Israel and the Temple was rebuilt and dedicated, with much rejoicing, in March of 515 BC (Ezra 6:13–18).[4] The second temple was not as grand as Solomon's. More important, the throne of David was not reestablished according to prophetic hope. With the exception of a brief period following the Maccabean rebellion, the Jews and their temple remained under foreign rule until the final destruction in

AD 70. Solomon built the original temple during the rise of Israel as a political power, which started during the reign of King David and continued under Solomon himself. After the exile that power was shattered. With a substantial proportion of Jews living outside Palestine, access to the temple was limited. These factors combined to permanently shift the focus of Israel's faith. Seeking God's presence through worship in the temple shifted to seeking his presence through reading sacred scriptures.

During the last two centuries before Christ, the Jewish people began to recognize a collection of writings as both authoritative and representative of God's ongoing presence among his people. The best-known part of this collection was the law, but other sacred literatures were collected and developed as well. The history of Judaism and its shift from temple to sacred text is certainly much more complex than I have laid out here, but for understanding how the early Christians came to view scripture, this is the critical development to keep in mind. It is extremely significant that the Christian understanding of the role and nature of scripture arose against this background and not in the modern world. The modern world is inclined to see the written word simply as the means of transmitting information. The foundation of the Christian understanding and use of scripture was rooted in an ancient Jewish context, which saw scripture not only as information but also as the place where one went to stand in the presence of God.

Monastic history

For the first eleven centuries of Christian history, God was encountered by reading, chanting, listening to, and praying with the scriptures. The use of the scriptures as a way of seeking the presence of God grew hand in hand with the rise of monasticism as a vital expression of radical Christianity. The monks had access to the scriptures, as most other people of that era did not, because they organized their lives around them. They read them and reread them, copied and recopied them. Copying the scriptures was a chief enterprise of monasteries up until the invention of the printing press. This wasn't a cottage industry to support the monks through the production of scripture copies; it was central to everything they were about. They dedicated themselves to the copying, reading, studying, singing, and praying of scripture because they were convinced that their spiritual lives depended on it.

This total dedication to the scriptures served not only the monks themselves but the rest of the church as well. From the third or fourth centuries until the twelfth, monasteries were the center of scripture study and teaching for the whole church. The monks did this study and teaching in order that people might find God and grow in holiness. With the rise of scholasticism in the twelfth century, the center of scripture study shifted from the monasteries to the university, where it has remained ever since.[5] With the shift came a major change in how the scripture is viewed and how it is used. The monk says to the scripture, "Lead me into loving unity with God." The scholar says, "Explain to me the nature of God and how he works." The monk sought to be in a love relationship with God. The scholar sought to understand God. Both are legitimate aims, but for anyone seeking to become holy, the monk's appeal must be primary. I am not at all against academics or the academic study of scripture. Much of my understanding of this whole topic is derived from the faithful labors of scholars. The essential point I am making is that we must continue to seek God himself in scripture. Scripture cannot be reduced to a source of information about God.

Principles of interpretation

Along with the move toward sacred texts as the center of the Jews' religious life came a growing appreciation of the text's deeper levels of meaning.[6] Since many of the texts were historical documents from cultures long gone, reporting events that were nearly as far from the experience of Jews in the second century BC as they are from ours, that historical distance—along with the philosophical influences of the Greeks[7]—contributed to various interpretations based on the discovery of hidden and allegorical meanings. Some of the hidden meanings were a departure from the faith of Israel, but mostly they were attempts to understand the ancient texts in a way that made sense in their contemporary world. Jews of the second temple period sought to find the presence of God in texts that didn't easily lend themselves to it.

Early Christians followed this practice as well. The Hebrew scriptures, which only much later came to be called the Old Testament, were their Bible. Believers continued to consider themselves Jews in some fundamental sense until persecution gradually widened the breach between them and their roots. They understood that Jesus was the pivotal point of history and sought to understand the Hebrew scriptures in light of Jesus. They naturally often resorted to looking for hidden meanings in the texts. As the early church began to gather a collection of sacred writings of their own, they continued with these same methods of interpretation. It was common for Christian interpreters to describe two or more levels of meaning in a text. Paul himself did this in Galatians 4, where he uses the biblical story of Hagar and Sarah as an allegory with a literal historical meaning and a deeper spiritual meaning. The literal account of the two women is used to describe the more profound spiritual significance of the old and new covenants. Origen, an influential interpreter in the early third century AD, described scripture interpretation in terms of using the tools of typology and allegory to discover what the Holy Spirit was teaching in the text. For the most part, this method of reading scripture didn't turn into a free-for-all of finding whatever readers wanted to find in the text. Rather, it usually became a way of shedding further light on what the church had already come to believe about Jesus and the calling of those who followed him.

One of the more interesting phenomena of seeking spiritual meanings in the texts of scripture was the use of the Song of Solomon. It was a favored source of deeper meaning for Christians and Jews alike.[8] Saint Bernard of Clairvaux, a twelfth-century Cistercian abbot, wrote eighty-six sermons on the Song (covering only up to Song of Sol. 3:4). Preached to his monks, these sermons are polished literary works. They tell of the love between Christ and individual Christians and Christ and his church.[9]

I don't raise this matter of spiritual levels of meaning in scripture for historical interest or to exhort anyone to go and do likewise. There are tremendous problems involved with this kind of interpretation, but that's just what makes it so interesting. One would have expected bad interpretation to bear bad fruit. For the most part, this loose interpretation did quite the opposite in the hands of the ancient monks. Rather than accepting the good results of allegorical interpretation as proof that this kind of exegesis is justified, I believe instead that one can be mistaken in exegesis and still

be led by the Spirit through the scripture if one has an open heart
to seek God himself.

There is one further insight I think we can draw from the ancient
monks and their allegorical interpretations of texts like the Song of
Solomon. They landed squarely on the one interpretive principle
that matters most—*God is love*. The Song of Solomon was not an
open field in which their speculative imaginations ran wild. It was
a story of a love relationship that could be interpreted in terms of
God's love for his people in a way that described how they actually
experienced God. Surrounded by many misguided influences, the
ancient monks sought the God whom they believed to be the source
of Love and came up knowing the only truth that matters. Their
clear example of seeking the true God (and not the philosophical or
interpretive methods of the past) inspires me to say, "*Pick up your
Bible and go and do likewise.*"

My purpose is certainly not to reduce the Bible to a devotional
tract. It is a source for ethics (how we should live), for theology
(what God is like, and how he works in the world), for ecclesiol-
ogy (what the church should look like and how it should function
in the world), for anthropology (what human beings are like and
how we got this way), and especially for soteriology (how we are
to be saved). If any of these things are to be seen truly, however,
they will be secondary to the desire for God himself. When we
come to the scripture with that desire primary and all desire for
other knowledge secondary, we are in a good position to receive
from God himself.

Even to the great saints and most holy readers of scripture, God
does not appear out of the pages of scripture like a pop-up picture
in a child's book, just as the priests who "inquired of the Lord"
in the temple rarely (I won't say never) spoke with a visible God
who appeared, talked audibly, and gave instructions. A person
would go to the temple and deal with the appointed staff of Levite
priests who were probably no more impressive than the members
of your church. Once in a great while, someone received a vision
in the temple, but most of the time nothing visibly supernatural
happened. Yet a sense of the reality of God's presence was available to those who came and inquired there with a sincere heart.
This is available for us as well if we approach the scripture with
the appeal, "Lead me into loving unity with God that I may be
conformed to his will."

Lectio Divina

Lectio divina, which literally means divine reading, was standard practice during most of the monastic period referred to above. This practice provided a guide for seeking God in the scriptures. Modern writers often describe it as a method of prayer. I am including it with the discussion of scripture because I believe it gives concrete direction for our effort to seek God—not just information—in the text. When the boundaries between scripture reading and prayer become very fuzzy, God is near.

Lectio divina was probably brought to the West from the Eastern desert fathers by John Cassian at the beginning of the fifth century. However, it has been closely connected to Saint Benedict whose blueprint for monastic life formed much of Western monasticism.[10] Traditionally, lectio divina is divided into four distinct parts, or movements, which are still often referred to by the Latin terms lectio, meditatio, oratio, and contemplatio. These mean something like: reading, reflection, prayer, and contemplation. The method of lectio divina is described by the twelfth-century Carthusian prior Guigo II as follows: "Reading, you should seek; meditating, you will find; praying, you shall call; and contemplating, the door will be opened to you."[11] A contemporary Southern rural minister, when asked how he prayed, replied: "I reads myself full; I thinks myself clear; I prays myself hot; I lets myself cool."[12]

Lectio (reading)

Lectio divina begins with simply reading some part of scripture. The portion used can be large or small; there is no prescription or formula for it. I often just read until it feels like I need to stop and think about it for a while.

Meditatio (meditation)

The word meditation in this context means putting your mind to what you have been reading and opening yourself to God in the process. For example, when I read John 1:5 I think about the light shining in the darkness, about Jesus coming into the world as the light of God. But I don't stop there. I go on to think about the darkness in my own soul, my struggles of light against darkness, and also the struggles in the souls of my brothers and sisters in the church. The image of light and darkness takes on a very personal meaning. What is usually called "Bible study" takes place in this step, as I search out the meaning of the text and open myself to what the implications are for me. For example, in meditating on this passage, I received an overwhelming personal assurance of the ultimate victory of light over darkness in my own case and that of several others in the church. This was not a private revelation. Through the Spirit's help I had simply grasped the implications of what I had read. You won't always receive that clear an illumination. Some texts obviously lend themselves more to it than others. The Spirit who is beyond our control is the one who guides us as we read.

The difficulty in finding the relevance of some texts can prod you to look for hidden meanings. I don't recommend that method, especially not if you tend toward believing that your imaginative interpretations are what the texts themselves mean. On the other hand, once you have tried to understand the texts, you can let your imagination run very freely and let the scriptural images or stories take root in you. While this step in *lectio divina* is a thinking step, it is not simply working out logical deductions. It will include that, but expect God occasionally to show you things you would not have seen through your own process of logical deduction. For example, while reading a passage in Second Chronicles about King Ahaziah of Judah being influenced by bad counsel to his ruin, I don't settle on thinking about Ahaziah's unfaithfulness. I don't want to just work out the practical teaching examples of giving and receiving advice. I feel the impact in terms of how ill-equipped I am to direct God's people even though I have often thought otherwise. That is not a teaching derived from interpreting this text. The Spirit is leading me to a sense of dependence and prayer. As for discerning what is the Spirit and what is my own vivid imagination, dependence and prayer are pretty safe indicators of the Spirit.

Oratio (prayer)

Prayer is the natural response to God that comes from being in his presence as we have read and reflected on the scripture. We naturally respond by calling out to God for his help for ourselves and others. Our plea naturally turns to praise for what he is doing.

Contemplatio (contemplation)

The meaning of contemplation as applied to Christian prayer has changed during the course of history. What Saint Bernard of Clairvaux meant by *contemplatio* and what Saint John of the Cross meant by it a few hundred years later aren't quite the same thing. I think it is best to understand contemplation as something like resting quietly in the presence of God. I like the "I lets myself cool" perspective quoted above. You have read, you have thought about what you have read, you have responded to God in prayer; now just sit there. Don't rush off to do something else as if you had something more important to do. It's hard to explain what to do in contemplation, because it is precisely not doing anything. Be in God's presence without babbling on about doing something, like Peter did at the transfiguration (Matt. 17:1–8; Mark 9:2–8; Luke 9:28–36).

Most of us have a lot in common with Peter. Don't be distraught if your mind is a clutter of irrelevant thoughts, but don't just give yourself over to the thoughts either. As they come, try to give them over to God. If this is hard, attempt it for three to five minutes but don't make a torture of it. God is present. That is a fact. In time you will grow increasingly conscious of it.

I find that I often move back and forth freely between these steps—you do not have to follow a prescribed order. Start with the reading part to give focus to the rest. If moving along in order helps, fine—but don't fight it if you find yourself doing otherwise on occasion. If I am reading a long passage of scripture, as I usually do when I am reading the historical books, I occasionally think about them as I go. That naturally leads to prayer, and so on, back and forth. Remember, *it is seeking God that is important, not the method.* The method is designed to get you prayerfully into the scriptures, where you will find God.

Eleven

Mysticism

My Lord God,
I have no idea where I am going.
I do not see the road ahead of me.
I cannot know for certain where it will end.
Nor do I really know myself,
 and the fact that I think that I am following your will
  does not mean that I am actually doing so.
But I believe that the desire to please You
 does in fact please You.
And I hope that I have that desire in all that I am doing.
I hope that I will never do anything apart from that desire.
And I know that if I do this,
 You will lead me by the right road
  though I may know nothing about it.
Therefore I will trust You always
 though I may seem to be lost
  and in the shadow of death.
I will not fear, for You are ever with me,
 and You will never leave me to face my perils alone.

Thomas Merton[1]

Jesus said to his first disciples that he would be with them always, even to the end of the age. He promised them he would send his Spirit to be with them, and that Spirit came on the gathered disciples at Pentecost. As the basis for his logic about Christian living and ethics, Paul assumes that those who are in Christ have the Spirit of Christ. It's not just Paul, either. The whole New Testament assumes that God is present with his people, the church. God's presence is not something isolated to the past or held off to the future. All Christian church denominations assume that God is present with his people in this present age. Our pursuit of holiness depends on God being present with us in this life and in this world.

God is with us, yet Christians are hungry for the presence of God! Most Christians do not understand how God is present. In spite of clear doctrinal beliefs about God's presence, most people do not often experience anything they recognize as such. Some Christian groups make claims of God's presence in charismatic gifts. They work hard in their worship services to generate emotions and other experiences that affirm it. Other groups are suspicious that this is manipulation and hold charismatic manifestations of the presence of God at arm's length. For them, no experiential evidence is expected or, at least officially, wanted. Both solutions, in the end, can leave people feeling empty and longing for something that feels more real. That emptiness can pull people toward a genuine seeking after God, but it can also pull the opposite way, tempting the human ego to assert its own transcendence.

The search for transcendence

One of the most basic elements of human nature is the instinct to try to transcend human limitations. We know that somehow we are more than animals, and yet we are limited to animal-type bodies. We feel ourselves to be of cosmic importance, yet are subject to decay and death. We rage against this unfairness.

> Do not go gentle into that good night
> Old age should burn and rave at close of day;
> Rage, rage against the dying of the light . . .[2]

Being human creatures unable to control our destiny is not enough. The serpent laid exactly this enticement before Eve in the Garden of Eden. His sales pitch for the forbidden fruit was that God was holding something back from her, and if she ate the fruit she would become like God, knowing good and evil. Religious experience is one of the most promising ways of trying to transcend the limitations of being human. It seems to put us in touch with something beyond the limited and limiting physical world, since the world of the supernatural is not subject to the limitations of the natural. The realm of unseen powers offers the enticing possibility of rising above the herd of humanity. One who is in touch with "the heavenly realms" and can draw on the power there is a long way ahead of the rest of humanity. So says the Serpent.

For a short period of human history, at least in the industrialized world, it seemed like science and technology could provide a way past the established limits of what human beings could do—and without even accessing the heavenly realms! We could see and hear around the world and even fly in space. Surely even the ultimate limitations of aging and death would fall before the rising power of human technology.

This optimism changed the way people saw the universe. As we explained more of the mechanics of living things, there was less need to reach into the supernatural realm to explain things. Advances in science enabled humanity to explain itself on a different basis: OK, so we *are* sophisticated monkeys, but we are getting more sophisticated all the time, evolving steadily toward mastering our environment. There really are no evil spirits lurking in the dark—or so we thought for a while—only mechanisms and processes that we are learning to control. There seemed much less need for God.

But it didn't work. The promise of transcendence by technology is a lie. Technology could only postpone or drag out the problem of death. Technology has produced some really cool video games, but human nature has remained a mess. There are street crimes, wars, and economic depressions. Families, pursuing the aspirations of a world set free from the supernatural, can't manage to live with each other in the same house. Husbands and wives can't stand to live with each other and neither can stand to live with their children. The children have become truly modern and seek to become gods by the age of fifteen, rejecting the parents and their world filled with limitations. Expanding economies enable some people to buy and buy, but life gets emptier and emptier. In the workplace people are not fulfilled, and the promise of shorter working hours not realized. Instead, people have become a part in a machine being pushed harder and harder. In spite of ever-expanding forms of entertainment, people increasingly find themselves bored and unhappy. Science and technology didn't have the answer. The promised fulfillment of being set free from the supernatural, from God himself, didn't happen.

When I became a Christian in 1971, the problem I faced in telling my friends was not justifying why I had come to believe in Jesus rather than some other religion. It was trying to explain why I believed in any supernatural realm at all. The physical universe was all there was to the people I knew then. That is no longer true for many. In the meantime, what is called "postmodernism" has set in. In the face of overwhelming evidence that atheistic science failed to bring us to transcendence, people began to lose their faith in it. It was an experiment doomed from the beginning, since it had no real solutions to offer.

Now as I encounter people, I rarely need to justify believing in the supernatural. They too believe. What they reject is the notion of a God to whom they must give an account. When a person ceases to believe in God, it is not that he or she then believes in nothing, but that he or she will believe anything.[3] Now that the god of scientific progress has lost some of its power, well-educated people believe in shamanism, in astrology, in anything. People create their own religions, seeking to transcend the limitations of being human creatures and asserting their own deity.

The reach for transcendence on the part of modern people isn't all rebellion. Human beings were created in the image of God and have a built-in longing for him. We all have a sense that we are spiritual beings in need of being nurtured by something beyond the visible world of science and technology. I once knew an intelligent professional person who was apprenticing herself to a Native American shaman. She believed that all religions are ultimately directed toward the same goal. I argued that the important distinction between religions was this: 1) Do you seek to worship God who is truly over us, or 2) do you seek to gain personal power by learning to control spiritual forces? To this she responded, "Oh, I'm not going to worship anything!"

Christians also long for contact with the unseen world, so it is not surprising that many of them are turning to an interest in mysticism. They are inclined to look in this direction for an experiential affirmation of their Christian faith, and there is within Christianity a rich mystical tradition to draw on. Many, though by no means all, of the saints have been mystics.

On the one hand, we can be thankful for this interest. People might seek God and worship him. On the other hand, interest in the supernatural presents the danger of seeking personal power and the worship of self. The latter is the natural bent of the sin that infects us. Most of the Christian mystics of the past were solidly rooted in the church with its traditions and doctrinal authority. Today, much of the popular interest is on the part of people with no such grounding. Without solid roots in the church, there is nothing to bring us up short when we head for the chasm of Self. By itself, the human desire for transcendence is a very poor guide to truth, and, in the realm of the mystical, truth must guide the way. Without truth, people will certainly get lost in themselves—or worse. Just as there are no saints outside the church, there is no legitimate Christian mysticism outside the church.

Defining Christian mysticism

There is no single agreed-upon definition of mysticism. In Eastern religions and often in their Western New Age imitations, the term is used to talk about the experiential realization of the oneness of all things. Sometimes people use "mysticism" on a popular level to include anything supernatural such as shamanism or occultism. People who study mysticism usually consider this an improper use of the term. Mysticism does not provide some undefined common ground shared by all religions. Putting this understanding of mysticism into its historical context, Bernard McGinn says,

> Mysticism is best seen not as some distinct or independent entity or form of religion but as an element in concrete religious communities and traditions. . . . We must remain conscious that the mystical element is part of a larger whole. . . . Christian mysticism can only be understood through the appropriation of its history.[4]

In plain language: Christian mysticism has to be understood as a part of the Christian faith and the church as it has existed in real history. Christian mysticism cannot be understood or experienced from an abstract "universal" perspective. You can only experience or understand Christian mysticism from the perspective of a life governed by faith in Jesus Christ and participation in his relationship with his Father, the God of Israel and of the church.

This needs to be spelled out because not all mystical claims made by Christian people are Christian in content. The central role of the teaching and doctrinal authority of scripture and the church cannot safely be set aside in favor of personal experience or speculation. There is a truly Christian mysticism, but it is not found by embracing everything mystical that comes along.

Seeking the experience of God's presence

There is nothing you can do directly to bring about a mystical experience. Trying to psychologically manipulate yourself to obtain it is a serious mistake. What you can and must seek after is holiness, the state of being undivided toward God. Holiness includes being content with whatever experiences God chooses to grant you—or not to grant you. You must grasp at nothing but what God freely gives you. In chapter 5 I talked about knowing God by pure faith. That is the central word to us about seeking to know God. Mystical experiences, like good feelings, are not the goal to be pursuing. If we turn our attention toward seeking after mystical experiences, we will be distracted from our goal of holiness. It is very important to keep the goal of holiness at the forefront when we consider the subject of mystical consciousness or any special experiences. If we seek special experiences rather than seeking to become holy, we will surely run ourselves into a spiritual ditch. We will not only be distracted from pursuing holiness, but we will inhibit genuine experiences of the presence of God as well. We have no reason to expect that we will encounter God if we refuse to follow his terms. In that case we will more likely fall into some sort of false mysticism or become discouraged and give up looking for God altogether.

Even though Christian mystics caution against seeking mystical states, they are clear that you can work at opening yourself to God in whatever way he presents himself to you. You do this by giving yourself fully to doing his will, and trusting in his goodness toward you. You don't open yourself to God by developing special powers of consciousness. In the previous chapter I pointed to a sound and traditional way Christians have sought God's presence in scripture. Certainly that is a means of seeking God's presence, but one that is focused on his revelation of himself in the scriptures given to the entire church.

We can give ourselves without reservation to serving him in the church. God is in fact present to us as we are a part of his church and seek to be conformed to his will. No special state of consciousness is required. Simple faith in God's promise of his presence can grow until mystical consciousness as a confirmation is of no importance. Saint Thérèse seems to have had mystical experiences through part of her life. Near the end of her life, though, she no longer had them. She grew in faith to the point where she claimed she preferred not having them so that she could love God by pure faith. She preferred this because she knew that was most pleasing to God, not because it felt better. Pleasing God had become her only goal. Saints have no other goal.

True mysticism

Scripture itself is the root of Christian mysticism. The writers of the New Testament, with different nuances, understood Jesus as the presence of God on earth and that he promised a continued presence with his first disciples and those who would come after. Christian mysticism in its roots goes back to this promise. The particular passages of scripture that may be understood as supporting various aspects of mysticism are of little importance in comparison with the promise of Jesus's ongoing presence. Legitimate Christian mysticism thus grows out of the expectation of Jesus's continuing presence with his church and not out of the innate human desire to reach for the heavens. This distinction between the experience of the Lord from within the church and the desire to transcend the human condition marks the divide between what I call true mysticism and false mysticism. The distinction is between the expectant creature hoping in God's promise and the "wannabe" god reaching for a place in the heavens. True mysticism is Christ-centered.[5] True mystical consciousness is not found in discovering the principle behind the universe, nor can we find it in the innate divinity of our own souls. Spiritual truth "discovered" through our own mystical experience apart from scripture or church tradition is simply coun-terfeit.[6] Mysticism in any Christian sense must ultimately answer to the scripture and the discernment of the church.

True mysticism is built on faith in Jesus Christ and participation in his church. It is not built on the cultivation of special abilities of the mystic. True mysticism turns a person ever deeper into de-pendence on Jesus and service to the church. It is never a means of appropriating supernatural powers of any kind. The mystic be-comes conscious of his or her oneness not only with Christ but also with the least of his or her brothers and sisters. There is never an affirmation of personal superiority. Christian mystics often have a sense of receiving a special gift, but it finds expression in humble service to the rest of the church, not in standing above the church. Consciousness of God's presence always brings humility and not pride. True mystical consciousness always moves a person to act in faith and love in the real world. Any mysticism that only leads to "other-worldliness" is false. Faith in action and love toward real people, not experiences or states of consciousness, are the litmus test for discerning true from false mysticism. "A tree is known by its fruit" (Matt. 12:33; Luke 6:44).

False mysticism

False mysticism is the ego's wishful thinking. It may also be a temptation of the evil one, but it is human pride at work that gives the devil a foothold in the soul. False mysticism comes from the desire to reach beyond the status of a humble creature dependent on God. The false mystic simply wishes to conform God to his or her own will rather than giving his or her own will over to God.

False mysticism can take a number of forms, from simply mistak-ing one's wishful thinking for a special word from God, to a real connection with the powers of evil. Likewise, a corresponding range of results can come about: anything from a temporary distraction from the goal of holiness to the ultimate disaster of turning away from Jesus. In between those extremes are spiritual experiences that turn one from simple obedience to a preoccupation with the excel-lence of one's self, which stops real spiritual growth in its tracks.

I am not concerned here with false mysticism that is motivated by the intentional pursuit of personal power. I assume that anyone reading this is not headed down that road. What I am saying is this: there is a whole range of mystical experience that Christians can get into that seems real but is not from God. These experiences are a substitute for real faith, not the fruit of faith. False mysticism is not hard to discern in yourself if you *want* to discern it, but the best route is to not seek after mystical experience at all. If you have what you consider a mystical experience, don't cling to it. If it is from God, it is in his control anyway. Set your attention fully on loving God with all your heart, mind, and soul, and your neighbor as yourself.

Mysticism and the church

Reading the writings of many of the ancient mystics, one becomes aware that the descriptions of mystical experience they describe seem to be profoundly individualistic. Mystical consciousness by its very nature is something that takes place within an individual. Even if a group of people had such an experience, it would still have to take place within individuals. A group of people could discuss such interior experiences to some degree, but the actual experience would still be at a personal level. This individuality has often been troubling to people whose concern is building up the church as a whole. For the most part, however, the concern remains a theoretical one rather than a real one. Mystical experience, if it is truly from God, *is* for the purpose of building up the church,[7] and it is striking how important Christian mystics have been in building up the church and calling it to faithfulness. This isn't to say that most great church leaders have been mystics, but most of the great mystics have also been leaders in the church in one way or another. Sometimes they have built up the church from inside the official organizational structure (Saint Augustine or Gregory the Great). Other times they have done it from outside the official leadership structure (Saint Francis). In either case they have been people who are loyal members of the church and who stood in submission to the church. Likewise, in our own times, we should be using any truly Christian mystical experience to turn people toward building up the church and not toward tearing it down.

Twelve

Prayer

Rejoice in hope, be patient in suffering, persevere in prayer.

Romans 12:12

It's a little embarrassing for me to confess that I don't actually have much to say on the topic of prayer. You would expect that someone who talks about becoming a saint would have a lot to say about prayer. When I hear of people spending long hours in fervent prayer I am usually a little suspicious or a little jealous. Either they are being disingenuous about the way they pray, or their ability in prayer reveals my failure (not that I'm comparing!). The inclination toward extended periods of praying has always escaped me. I don't think I am the only one for whom this is true. I learned a long time ago, as a new pastor fresh out of seminary, that if I wanted to preach a sermon that would make people feel a bit guilty, all I had to do was preach about how we ought to pray a lot. The hypocrisy of preaching such sermons finally got to me, so I gave it up permanently.

Saying that we ought to try to pray a little, rather than not at all, would be more helpful to most of us. Most of us are driven to pray fervently at some points in our lives. This happens naturally when we find ourselves or our loved ones in crisis and we desperately need help. But even then, the length of time spent in single focused prayer is relatively small. Because we can't pray for long stretches, even in a crisis, we feel like failures, but the sense of failure does nothing to motivate us to act differently except in brief spurts of resolve that quickly fade.

My purpose in writing this chapter is to point a way through this guilt-approach to the topic. First, I want to clarify what my understanding of prayer is. Second, I want to provide a perspective that allows a person to move forward in prayer rather than remaining in the paralysis that is so common.

What is prayer?

Our prayer is a participation in Jesus's own relationship with his Father. While on Earth, Jesus's relationship with his Father was one of constant prayer. Everything he did he received from his Father. "Jesus said to them [the Jews], 'Very truly, I tell you, the Son can do nothing on his own, but only what he sees the Father doing; for whatever the Father does, the Son does likewise'" (John 5:19). In this way he carried out his Father's will and not his own will, even to the point of death on the cross (Luke 22:42). Jesus's relationship to his Father was carried on by means of prayer. His prayer was set in a relationship of complete openness to his Father's will without imposing any conditions of his own. He only asked his Father for things that were in accordance with his Father's will—in effect, he was only asking for help in carrying out his Father's will. He did not seek his own glory in anything, but only the glory of the Father (John 7:16–18, 8:50; Heb. 5:5).

The basis of our prayer is not that we have a rich father who only wants to hear us ask before he gives us what we want. Our basis for prayer is that we are included in Jesus. The Father hears us because we are included in Jesus's dedication to the Father's will. For us, praying rightly is participating in Jesus's own prayer, which always serves the Father's will. "And this is the boldness we have in him, that if we ask anything according to his will, he hears us" (1 John 5:14). In our desire to pray we must concentrate not on methods of prayer or even disciplines of prayer but on adopting Jesus's attitude toward the Father. We must learn to seek his will, not our own—his glory rather than our own.

The Apostle Paul admonishes that we should "pray without ceasing" (1 Thess. 5:17). It seems to me that we can take this in one of three ways. Either 1) he is just being hyperbolic, using "without ceasing" to mean frequently or regularly, 2) he is asking something beyond the capability of virtually everyone, or 3) he means something different from the conventional formal act of praying words to God, whether mentally or audibly. My conclusion is the last, that he means something different, quite different. After all, there are only so many words one can say to anyone, especially day after day. Even the best of talkers can hardly "talk without ceasing," though most of us have known people who seem to try. There must be more to it.

Prayer of the heart

As we struggle on in hope, longing for our full redemption, the Holy Spirit himself prays within us.

> . . . the Spirit helps us in our weakness; for we do not know how to pray as we ought, but that very Spirit intercedes with sighs too deep for words. And God, who searches the heart, knows what is the mind of the Spirit, because the Spirit intercedes for the saints according to the will of God. (Rom. 8:26–27)

The result is prayer welling up from within. It may be what the Psalmist experiences when he prays,

> Deep calls to deep at the thunder of your cataracts; all your waves and your billows have gone over me. By day the LORD commands his steadfast love, and at night his song is with me, a prayer to the God of my life. (Ps. 42:7–8)

There is a Russian spiritual classic called *The Way of a Pilgrim*,[1] a folk story of a man who sets out to learn to pray without ceasing. He is counseled by a wise man to simply pray, "Lord Jesus Christ, have mercy on me" over and over again.[2] He sets out on a pilgrimage walking about the country repeating this prayer constantly. At first it is a mechanical repetition. It becomes much more than that; eventually he no longer needs to think of saying it. It becomes a part of his being, and an evidence of the transformation toward holiness he is undergoing. The prayer takes root in his heart. What is involved here has first to do with calling on Jesus and second with a serious attempt at keeping oneself consciously centered in God.

John Cassian gave similar counsel with regard to continuous prayer. He passed on the wisdom of the Desert Fathers that in order to keep the thought of God always in your mind you should persistently pray this formula: "God, come to my assistance. Lord, make haste to help me."[3]

In both of these cases the method is first an appeal to God based on constant need, and second, a discipline for learning to remain centered on the goal of living in and for God. It is an appeal to God, in faith, and a determined effort not to be distracted from the goal. Both *The Way of a Pilgrim* and John Cassian, in their different ways, affirm that as a person makes this appeal to God and struggles toward the goal, the Holy Spirit takes over and a new and deeper level of prayer arises from the heart. The goal of both is opening the soul to the Holy Spirit who effects the transformation of the person into holiness. The prayer is not an appeal for the Spirit to aid in my personal perfection; it is inviting the Spirit to live his life in me. The Spirit's prayer becomes my prayer. Or should I say my prayer becomes the Spirit's prayer? The distinction no longer exists. In the Eastern Church tradition this is called the "prayer of the heart." In this prayer a person is in communion with God in a passive state and not engaged in some kind of "work" of praying. The prayer of the heart is an expression of living in and for God. Prayer without ceasing is the Spirit himself set free within us.

It is important to note that both the story of the pilgrim and the teachings of John Cassian are given to people who have decided to give their lives fully to God and are sincerely looking for how to do that. They are people who have already gotten past step one toward sainthood: they have decided to go for it. For them, the practical advice about prayer is the same as the practical advice about the whole of the spiritual life: expect God to act in you to accomplish the good he intends, and start acting accordingly—to the best of your limited ability. The Jesus prayer is one way of acting according to the best of your limited ability. It is not a magic formula for getting yourself into a mystical state. It is simply a feeble but sincere attempt to learn to pray without ceasing.

Perspective on prayer

One of the ways that prayer gets derailed is when we imagine that, in prayer, we must somehow scale the heavens with the eloquence of our words or the fervent intensity or quality of our prayer. True prayer arises from knowing ourselves as children of a good and loving Father. We are sitting in our heavenly Father's lap. More than that, we have his Spirit within us, and we are in him. We do not pray as outsiders. We are insiders with God. From this place, prayer can become a deep mystery of loving communication within a spiritual unity that transcends human comprehension. We pray from the deep center of love within God himself, a place where we have no right to be. We are there because that is where his love for us has placed us. For this reason the prayer of the heart overflows into adoration, which is "the last effort of a soul that has flooded its banks and can speak no more."[4]

I realize that this would appear to be describing some kind of profound mystical experience. I suppose the consciousness of this prayer of the heart or prayer in the spirit could be called mystical, but that is not my point. For one who is in Christ, this "participation in the divine nature" (see 2 Pet. 1:4) is simply a fact, whether one is immediately conscious of it or not.

"Ordinary" prayer

Something as mundane as saying words of petition and praise as an act of discipline may seem like a move backward from the exalted state of prayer I just described. You may think we are back to where we started, facing the difficulty of praying when we don't feel like doing it. Actually, this "ordinary" prayer is not ordinary at all. Ordinary prayer is as mystical as what I have been describing above. When we make petitions for ourselves or others we may feel like nothing is happening, but in fact the Holy Spirit is praying within us just as surely as in any other state of prayer. In fact, when we intercede with him for our brothers and sisters we come most closely to the intention of God's love. When we give thanks and praise it gladdens our Father's heart.

The desire for the mystical is prevalent in our times, and people are often tempted to give up "ordinary" prayer altogether and pursue mystical or contemplative prayer instead. This is a serious mistake. Mystical or contemplative prayer is no substitute for "ordinary" prayer. On the contrary, real Christian mystics have strict disciplines of "ordinary" prayer.

The natural question at this point is, Why does God want us to ask him for things anyway? He already knows our needs. Surely we are not going to persuade him to do something he doesn't intend to do. He knows our hearts, so why do we need to put our praise and thanksgiving into words? The various theological explanations don't seem very convincing or motivating to me. Jacques Ellul's argument—that we should pray for no other reason than the fact that we have been commanded to[5]—should be sufficient, but it is not very inspiring. Given who God is, there must surely be a reason for prayer besides an arbitrary command. Not surprisingly, Saint Thérèse has a perspective that I have found helpful. She says, "God wishes to do nothing without us."[6] She simply assumes God loves us so much that he wants to include us in what he is doing. No further theological speculation is required. It pleases God for us to pray because he enjoys our participation with him.

If Thérèse is right, and she is surely right in at least her attitude, the nature of what we are up to as we try to pray is changed. Prayer is no longer about us and our disciplined performance or lack of it. Our effort in prayer is for the purpose of giving joy to God as we join him in his work. Prayer with this attitude is participation in Jesus's relationship with his father. That is worth putting some effort into. We don't have to do all-night prayer vigils once a week. God isn't impressed by our spiritual athletics. What we need to do is pray with joy and gratitude and not just ignore the invitation to work side by side with God.

The root or the fruit?

We may easily assume that prayer is a means to spiritual growth and therefore we must work hard at it to climb our way up. From my own experience, I am more inclined to say that prayer grows naturally out of the simple desire to live in and for God.[7] That is certainly the way Jesus approached it. For us, prayer is the fruit of spiritual growth at least as much as it is a means to it. Discipline is not enough to start the fire, but once the fire is started one can learn some discipline.

To the extent that I really want to live in and for God, I also genuinely want to pray. When I say "want to" I am distinguishing it from "feel like." The distinction is important. If I want to pray but don't feel like it at the moment, discipline is directed at doing something I want to do rather than something I don't really want to do. If I really do not want to pray, rather than trying to discipline myself to pray, I need to go back and again take hold of my decision to live in and for God. Disciplines of prayer are important from that decision point on, but it isn't where I start. Turning back from giving myself fully to God, not problems of concentration or time or anything else, is the central cause of prayerlessness. I have to start by deciding to give myself over to God himself on his own terms. There is no way forward in prayer if I am thinking that prayer is a way of getting something from God without giving myself fully to his will.

Thirteen

Possessions and Money

Do not be afraid, little flock, for it is your Father's good pleasure to give you the kingdom.

Luke 12:32

Whenever one thinks of saints, one usually thinks of austerity. The question of money and possessions always comes up. The best known of the canonized saints were known for their rejection of all worldly goods, and Jesus himself was notable for not having many worldly goods.

Much of the impetus behind the actions of saints comes from their intention to imitate Jesus. Saint Francis is the most notable example. He set out to consciously imitate Jesus, and he understood this in terms of suffering and poverty. Francis was probably more extreme about this than Jesus himself was. As Jesus traveled about on his itinerant ministry he seems to have accepted hospitality from a variety of people, including some of at least modest wealth. Saint Francis once went to Rome on some business with the Vatican and while there refused the hospitality offered to him. Instead, he went out and begged bread on the street. I have no idea whether this was always his practice or not, but it was clear that he was trying to make a point. Poverty was clearly central to what Francis was up to. Poverty became, in some sense, his gospel. It is not at all clear that poverty was central to what Jesus was up to.

Some readers will be anxious to point out that there is a legitimate biblical strand of teaching that sets poverty up as a spiritual ideal. It comes from Israel's prophets who were appalled at the exploitation of the poor by the rich among the people of God. In this perspective, poverty is certainly not idealized—just the opposite. Poverty should not happen among the people of God! In Acts we see there were no poor people among the early Christians because they were sharing all their possessions with each other (Acts 4:34). This was a sign that the kingdom of God was present.

The prophets establish a very close relationship between idolatry and poverty. In the New Testament, Paul reaffirms this in his statement that "greed is idolatry" (see Col. 3:5). The prophets saw that God's holy nature demands that he come to the aid of the poor. God takes zealous action both for his name and for the sake of the poor. The name of the Lord and the poor are directly connected and set in opposition to the rich, who are proud and haughty. The rich have taken an arrogant attitude toward God and the poor simultaneously (i.e., Zeph. 3:11b–13a). Poverty is the condition of helplessness before arrogance and injustice, and it draws God's attention and favor. The concept of spiritual poverty arises out of the fact that those who are impoverished by injustice are humiliated. They are the ones who turn to God as their only source of help. In this context, the terms "poor" and "humble" become virtually synonymous. What the prophets set up as a positive ideal is not poverty as such but the humility that cries out to God in need.

The biblical line of logic seems quite different from the anti-materialism we see in Saint Francis. I am not trying to denigrate Saint Francis. He was formed by his own age as we are by ours, and he gave himself fully to God's will, as he understood it. Giving yourself fully to God is what makes a saint, not having a perfect understanding of the history of ideas. The only reason I think this point is worth making at all is that the idealization of poverty or even humility can take some very bad turns. (I'm not suggesting that Francis made those bad turns.) Human perversity can turn poverty and humility into a form of pride by claiming them as a kind of personal purity that gives a person standing over others. The history of both Judaism and Christianity are filled with examples. Once a person or group adopts the view that poverty is a virtue and classifies themselves as poor, praise of God becomes an occasion for self-congratulation, and love of others deteriorates into judgment.[1] If poverty is kept in its biblical perspective, this distortion is less likely to happen.

Jesus on possessions and money

In spite of what I have said about Saint Francis's tendencies, let's not write him off too easily. If he was stretching the teaching of Jesus in idealistic directions, he was on more solid ground than people who cling to riches. Jesus's teaching on the topic of riches is very clear: "No one can serve two masters; for a slave will either hate the one and love the other, or be devoted to the one and despise the other. You cannot serve God and wealth" (Matt. 6:24). This doesn't logically exclude the theoretical possibility of a person being rich without serving wealth. But talking about wealth doesn't get to the heart of the matter for most people, because very few people consider themselves wealthy. Most of us think we are just getting by. Wealth is a relative term. One is wealthy or not in comparison with others, and in the capitalist/consumer culture of the affluent West most people usually make their comparisons upward. Consumer culture requires a built-in dissatisfaction with what one has.

Jesus has a much bigger understanding of wealth than the comparative analysis of consumer culture. He doesn't give much encouragement to people who want to justify any kind of a business-as-usual view of money and possessions.

I think Richard Hays gets at the heart of Jesus's concerns in his discussion of Luke-Acts.[2] Of the four Gospels, Luke's portrays Jesus in the most hard-line posture toward money and possessions. In Luke's version of the Beatitudes there is no spiritualizing as in Matthew. The materially poor and hungry are blessed and the rich are condemned. Jesus tells the rich young ruler to go sell everything, and give the money to the poor, as a condition of discipleship. When he declines the invitation, Jesus lets him go (Luke 18:18–30). On the other hand, Zacchaeus spontaneously repents and offers to give half his possessions to the poor as well as returning fourfold everything he has cheated anyone out of (Luke 19:1–10). Jesus responds to this with "Today salvation has come to this house." There is no standard requirement for the total renunciation of possessions. Hays concludes: In Luke-Acts, possessions "function as symbols of response to God. Zacchaeus's uncoerced generosity is a sign of repentance and faith, whereas the hesitant stinginess of the rich ruler—or, worse, the dishonesty of Ananias and Sapphira (Acts 5:1–11)—betrays an unrepentant heart, closed toward the grace of God."[3]

Money and possessions were important topics in Jesus's teaching, and he didn't waste much time accumulating them. Yet, Jesus does not seem to be interested in money or possessions in the same way Saint Francis is. They are not an evil to be avoided but a symbol of a person's response of openness to God. The picture we get here is a very different one from spurning the material world in favor of the spiritual world. Jesus calls for *generosity and openness*, not renunciation. The background of Jesus's attitudes about money and possessions is not renouncing worldly things, but the joyful, open giving to the Lord we see in King David's attitude. In First Chronicles 29 we see David making provision for the future building of the temple of the Lord by generous, joyful offerings of his own and inviting all the people to do the same. The people respond with freewill generosity and there is joy all around. David says,

> But who am I, and what is my people, that we should be able to make this freewill offering? For all things come from you, and of your own have we given you. For we are aliens and transients before you, as were all our ancestors; our days on the earth are like a shadow, and there is no hope. O LORD our God, all this abundance that we have provided for building you a house for your holy name comes from your hand and is all your own. (1 Chron. 29:14–16)

What Jesus wants is a full and glad response to God, whose kingdom he is announcing. If he has no place to lay his head, it is because he is preoccupied with doing his Father's will. He has the same attitude about food. When his disciples, realizing he hadn't eaten in quite a while, urged him to eat he said, "I have food to eat that you do not know about." After some more food discussion he clarified, "My food is to do the will of him who sent me and to complete his work" (John 4:31–34). A glad and open response to God underlies everything Jesus does and teaches. Grateful freedom permeates everything. He is not calling for an austerity program. We are to live in light of the truth that we are not our own but God's, and he is all love toward us. We are to have little attachment to wealth because we are so preoccupied with God's goodness and doing good for others that money is no longer a primary value for us.

What Jesus has no patience for is a tight-fisted grasping of wealth in the face of the goodness and generosity of God. This is the source of condemnation of the rich. That is, in general, how the rich behave. I have a friend who is a small building contractor. He finds it difficult to work for rich people. They are usually the ones who are hardest to get money out of. They love their money.

Before you say you are not too rich, remember that you are in a culture that, more than any other culture in the history of humankind, looks to money and possessions to give meaning to life. Personal affluence offers itself as an alternative to the kingdom of God. None of us escapes it untouched. If we are to be different from the culture around us, we will have to repent and grow in a different direction. Simply declaring oneself uncontaminated is most likely just a confession of blindness. The only way to ascertain growth in this area is seeing an increase in your openhandedness.

Another aspect of Jesus's concern with money had to do with how people treated other members of God's people. Jesus stands in the line of the Old Testament prophets on this subject. Jesus's parable of the rich man and Lazarus, for example, is a juxtaposition of a rich child of Abraham having no regard for the most basic needs of a poor brother. Jesus's views on this are reflected in the statement of 1 John: "How does God's love abide in anyone who has the world's goods and sees a brother or sister in need and yet refuses help?" (1 John 3:17). When the apostle Paul is appealing to the Corinthian church for money to help the church in Jerusalem, he says,

> I do not mean that there should be relief for others and pressure on you, but it is a question of a fair balance between your present abundance and their need, so that their abundance may be for your need, in order that there may be a fair balance. As it is written, "The one who had much did not have too much, and the one who had little did not have too little." (2 Cor. 8:13–15)

Here he is referring to God's feeding Israel in the wilderness during the exodus. Some have argued that Paul waters down Jesus's teaching on money. Actually, he is taking a pastoral stance on the topic, rather than a prophetic stance as Jesus did. He isn't watering down Jesus; he is getting at the heart of something Jesus was saying and putting it in terms of its practical implications for the church. And don't think this isn't radical. Can you imagine how different the church would be if it practiced this even within individual congregations! What if we practiced it with other congregations that were closest to our own beliefs? And what if we practiced it with other congregations across national boundaries? No, this doesn't reduce the radical nature of Jesus's teaching on money. Paul moves it from the abstract discussions that have so often confused the matter and puts it where Jesus intended it to be. "You shall love the Lord your God with all your heart, and with all your soul, and with all your strength, and with all your mind; and your neighbor as yourself" (Luke 10:27).

You may think that I have still not addressed the really hard sayings of Jesus such as: "So therefore, none of you can become my disciple if you do not give up all your possessions" (Luke 14:33). Let's look at it in context:

> Now large crowds were traveling with him; and he turned and said to them, "Whoever comes to me and does not hate father and mother, wife and children, brothers and sisters, yes, and even life itself, cannot be my disciple. Whoever does not carry the cross and follow me cannot be my disciple. For which of you, intending to build a tower, does not first sit down and estimate the cost, to see whether he has enough to complete it? Otherwise, when he has laid a foundation and is not able to finish, all who see it will begin to ridicule him, saying, 'This fellow began to build and was not able to finish.' Or what king, going out to wage war against another king, will not sit down first and consider whether he is able with ten thousand to oppose the one who comes against him with twenty thousand? If he cannot, then, while the other is still far away, he sends a delegation and asks for the terms of peace. So therefore, none of you can become my disciple if you do not give up all your possessions." (Luke 14:25–33)

I suppose this could be considered a hard teaching, but I want to point out two relevant factors. First, it can only be understood in the context of the kingdom of God, which Jesus is proclaiming and embodying. The demand is no different from what he teaches in the parable about the person who finds a treasure in a field and sells everything he has to buy this field (Matt. 13:44). He is clearly saying that being a part of the kingdom means giving up everything to get it. He is not merely asking for austerity, but rather inviting us to the joy of finding a great treasure. He teaches the same in the well-known parable of the wineskins (Mark 2:22; also Matt. 9:17; Luke 5:37–39). You can't put new wine in old wineskins. It would simply burst the old skin. You need to get a new wineskin to hold the new wine. The expectation is that getting a new skin is something worth doing, not a great sacrifice, and this is what Jesus is saying in the hard line of Luke 14:25–33. This "hard saying" is actually good news. Don't compromise the good news by trying to hang onto stuff that doesn't work in the kingdom of God. Gerhard Lohfink points out that in the parable of a man finding a treasure in a field, Jesus doesn't simply compare the kingdom of God to the treasure. He compares the kingdom to the whole process of finding the treasure and selling everything to buy the field. Jesus is talking about how the kingdom of God comes. The emphasis is not on selling everything but on the joy of finding the treasure. It isn't hard to sell everything. He is making the deal of a lifetime![4]

What Jesus is saying in Luke 14:25–33 is nothing more demanding than what I have been saying about becoming a saint. Being a saint is being undivided toward God, so don't let any of this old stuff get in the way. Being a saint is living in and for God, so why do you want to grasp at things as if you lived somewhere else? "Why do you spend your money for that which is not bread, and your labor for that which does not satisfy?" (Isa. 55:2). Jesus is just pointing out the things that we often want to make compromises about. We act as if we want to be commuters, living in God but keeping an office someplace else. Jesus says no to that. Everything I have been advocating about holiness says no to that. Yet holiness is what God requires of us, and he can make it happen if we are willing. Money and possessions are not a special category—they are just part of the furniture of our lives. This is no austerity program—quite the opposite. There is no greater reward than what God offers, and no greater joy either. Our anxiety over what the radical pursuit of sainthood might mean for our money and possessions is simply an indication that we are still trying to make compromises. That is why in the discussion of sainthood the topic of money always comes up. Money and possessions are indicators. We will not become holy by divesting ourselves of all of our possessions. To the extent we have become holy we will not be trying to cling to money, possession, pride, status, time, or anything else. "Do not be afraid, little flock, for it is your Father's good pleasure to give you the kingdom" (Luke 12:32).

FOURTEEN

DISCERNMENT

> Do not be conformed to this world, but be transformed by the re-
> newing of your minds, so that you may discern what is the will of
> God—what is good and acceptable and perfect.
>
> Romans 12:2

That we need to be undividedly dedicated to God's will is clear.
But we still need to make concrete decisions continually about our
individual and collective lives. Undividedness toward God's will
is not just an abstraction. We must actually seek to do his will in its
particulars. Those who seek to do God's will are the ones able to
recognize his word and his will (John 7:17).

Let us return to the heartbeat of this book: what God wants from
us is holiness. Holiness is being undivided toward God's will,
fully giving ourselves over into his hands and ceasing to keep one
hand on the controls ourselves. Undividedness means ceasing to
guard ourselves against the chance that God will steer us into a
precarious position. As we live into the knowledge that God's will
is good and perfect, our own will becomes so only insofar as we
conform it to his. Our *desire and intention* is to live in and for God
himself. This does not require perfection on our part. What God

wants from us has to do with intention and attitude more than with doing any particular thing right—with our sincere movement in his direction.

From this perspective, discerning God's will is easy for two reasons. First, it is easy because we are eliminating the biggest interference with discernment—*our assumption that it is to our advantage to keep our own interest in our own hands.* Second, since we are wanting God's will, he will certainly guide us in the way he wants us to go. To assume otherwise would be to think of God as an arbitrary and unloving parent who refuses to give his child direction but becomes angry when the child doesn't accurately guess what he intended. Our God is our loving father, not the capricious monster of the pagans. "Is there anyone among you who, if your child asks for a fish, will give a snake instead of a fish?" (Luke 11:11). Much of the anxiety over discerning God's will seems to ignore this obvious fact. We will not always comprehend his directions or have psychological certainty about what he wants. I am simply saying that *he will guide us into doing his will insofar as we sincerely continue to seek to do his will.* This simple claim is in fact a very powerful one and is the core assumption of spiritual discernment.

Spiritual discernment then has more to do with determination to give ourselves over to God than it does with figuring out which of the various courses of action God wants us to take. The only "discerning," in the sense of detecting, we have to do is to see when we are seeking to reassert our own will rather than to participate in God's. If we take the controls into our own hands, we will run ourselves into a ditch. Otherwise we are in good hands.

Discernment is a function of holiness

When considering how people discerned God's will in the Old Testament, it is natural to think in particular of the kings of Israel and Judah consulting prophets or being confronted by prophets with the word of the Lord. While these things happened and were important in the history of Israel, they are not what we would call discernment. They were a direct speaking of the word of God. There was nothing to discern, and the Old Testament texts do not speak of this process as discernment. Where the language of discernment is used extensively is within the wisdom tradition.

In ancient Israel, Solomon became the symbol of wisdom, known far and wide through the ages for his discernment. Soon after Solomon had become king, God appeared to Solomon in a dream and asked him what request he would like to make. (This is an opportunity far better than a genie coming out of bottle and granting three wishes.) Rather than asking for any of the usual things one would expect from a young king, Solomon asked for an understanding mind and the ability to discern between good and evil in order to govern God's people. This was a very clear statement of his desire to do God's will rather than steer his own course toward being a great king. God was pleased with this request and said,

> Because you have asked this, and have not asked for yourself long life or riches, or for the life of your enemies, but have asked for yourself understanding to *discern* what is right, I now do according to your word. Indeed I give you a wise and *discerning mind*; no one like you has been before you and no one like you shall arise after you. (1 Kings 3:11–12; emphasis added)

This didn't mean that God was promising to give Solomon a secret message on each matter that came to him. Instead, Solomon seems to have been given the ability to see life and its situations truly. Later in his life, with regard to foreign wives, Solomon began to assert his own autonomous will, and this led him to make a mess of things. Nevertheless, insofar as Solomon is held up as a model of wisdom and discernment, it is because he sought to be conformed to God's will, from the heart, rather than pursue the autonomous self-interest typical of kings.

In the above passage, the word "to discern" is the same Hebrew word *shema*, which also means "to hear" or "to listen." The same word is used when God says "obey" as in "Obey my voice."[1] Solomon has asked for understanding "to listen to what is right," "to obey what is right." There is more going on here than the granting of a special gift for moral detective work. The request and the gift are for understanding in order to obey.

Hearing as obeying is rooted in the very fabric of God's covenant relationship with Israel. The best known use of this word *shema* is in Deuteronomy: "Hear, O Israel: The LORD is our God, the LORD alone. You shall love the LORD your God with all your heart, and with all your soul, and with all your might" (Deut. 6:4–5). This passage has become known as the *Shema* after this very word we are discussing. It is the central and most important hearing/obeying that Israel has to do. The *Shema* is the call to Israel to be undivided toward their God. Obedient listening is the foundation of discernment. Solomon stands on that foundation when he asks for and is granted the "understanding to discern what is right."

Discernment is not just a translation of hearing and obeying. In the same sentence about Solomon, we have God's response: "I give you a wise and *discerning* mind." Here the word which the NRSV translates "discerning" is a different Hebrew word, one that is most often translated "understanding." The NRSV is not wrong in letting these two words appear interchangeable in translation. In the thought of ancient Israel, the concepts of discerning, knowing, understanding, hearing, and obeying God all run together as a single stream. Trying to separate them impedes the ability to discern, know, understand, hear, or obey.

The New Testament carries on this relationship of discernment to obedience. Discernment is never a matter of trying to detect the will of God. Discernment is directly correlated to giving oneself over to God and being transformed by him. When one is transformed, the will of God becomes obvious.

> I appeal to you therefore, brothers and sisters, by the mercies of God, to present your bodies as a living sacrifice, holy and acceptable to God, which is your spiritual worship. Do not be conformed to this world, but be transformed by the renewing of your minds, so that you may discern what is the will of God—what is good and acceptable and perfect. (Rom. 12:1–2)

As in the case of Solomon, discernment doesn't have to do with special instructions on specific matters but a recognition of "what is good and acceptable and perfect." Discernment is not seen as a discovery or a special message about an otherwise obscure will of God. It is simply the understanding granted to those who have not obstructed their vision with their own worldly will but have allowed God to renew their minds. It is wisdom that comes with undividedness toward God, a kind of *spiritual common sense*. While at times in both the New and the Old Testaments people get special directions from God, this is not what is referred to or expected when the language of discernment is used. The mind is not bypassed in favor of some other process, and special insider information is not the expectation.

The mind has a deservedly bad reputation. Luther talked about "that whore reason"[2] and sought to get it out of the loop of how we acquire spiritual knowledge. Given the history of what he saw the church doing, he wasn't being foolish. The Apostle Paul, however, saw the mind in need of transformation, not excommunication.

The mind needs renewing, and that happens only as we offer ourselves fully to God, seeking no compromise to keep one foot in the world. When we live in and for God, our reason becomes a useful tool for discernment. Reason without holiness is surely the whore that Luther called it, not a resource for understanding. Discernment involves the mind.[3] Rejecting reason doesn't result in spiritual discernment but in being pushed to and fro by our most deceptive whims of emotion and imagination.

Discernment is a kind of spiritual common sense, but the word "spiritual" is not just a descriptive word like the word "blue" placed before the word "car." If we are talking about a car, adding the word blue might help us distinguish it from a yellow car, but even without naming a color we would be clear on the nature of the thing we were talking about. If we were to subtract the word "spiritual" from the phrase "spiritual common sense," we would change the nature of the thing entirely. What is involved is not mindless. We have much more than our minds to use. We have God's own Spirit. First Corinthians is stunningly clear on this:

> But, as it is written, "What no eye has seen, nor ear heard, nor the human heart conceived, what God has prepared for those who love him"—these things God has revealed to us through the Spirit; for the Spirit searches everything, even the depths of God. For what human being knows what is truly human except the human spirit that is within? So also no one comprehends what is truly God's except the Spirit of God.
>
> Now we have received not the spirit of the world, but the Spirit that is from God, so that we may understand the gifts bestowed on us by God. And we speak of these things in words not taught by human wisdom but taught by the Spirit, interpreting spiritual things to those who are spiritual. Those who are unspiritual do not receive the gifts of God's Spirit, for they are foolishness to them, and they are unable to understand them because they are *spiritually discerned*. *Those who are spiritual discern all things*, and they are themselves subject to

no one else's scrutiny. "For who has known the mind of the Lord so as to instruct him?" But we have the mind of Christ. (1 Cor. 2:9–16; emphasis added)

"Those who are spiritual" seems to be another way of describing those who, in the language of Romans, live according to the Spirit and not according to the flesh. They are those who are on God's road to holiness. This is not just a catchall term for everyone who claims to be a Christian. Paul said that the Corinthian Christians were unspiritual and needed to start over (1 Cor. 3:1). What they couldn't therefore discern were the incredible gifts that God has bestowed on us in Jesus. The problem wasn't that they couldn't figure out some practical matter of church policy. They had lost sight of what Jesus had done for them and what he was intending to make them into. Consequently, they were competing and quarreling like undisciplined children (1 Cor. 3:3).

When we comprehend what we have been given in Jesus, our view of life is transformed. Our minds are renewed. It is impossible to have a glimpse of what is offered in Jesus and still cling to my own agenda rather than God's. But God's agenda is from another realm and can't be grasped with human reason alone. It has to be revealed by the Spirit, and when we grasp it we see everything in a new light—including ourselves. Paul continues in Romans 12 about discernment: "For by the grace given to me I say to everyone among you not to think of yourself more highly than you ought to think, but to think with sober judgment, each according to the measure of faith that God has assigned" (Rom. 12:3).

Spiritual discernment points us to God and away from ourselves. When we really live in that reality, we are living as saints. To the extent that we live as saints, we will have spiritual common sense. To the extent that we have spiritual common sense, we live as saints.

Hans Urs von Balthasar talks about spiritual attunement. This language is used to talk about the whole person—reason, will, and spirit—becoming attuned to God.[4] I am reminded of my first try at tuning a guitar and being quite unable to do it. Then I was shown how to adjust the tension on a string until it vibrated with the sound of one next to it. Discernment cannot be reduced to a checklist one goes through. It is learning to resonate with God.

A practical guide to personal decision making

Spiritual discernment always points to what God is doing in Jesus. It doesn't spell out where to go to college or what job to take. In the light of what God is doing in Jesus, where you go to college or what job you take becomes a very secondary matter. If you want to know God's will with regard to a particular decision you must make, don't separate your decision from your desire to become holy. If you have no intention of seriously trying to become holy, never mind trying to "discover" God's will.

I am not attempting to be cute or harsh but rather to be clear about the matter of discernment. The matter is that simple. If you are seeking holiness, you are seeking what God wants to give you, and he will direct you into the fullness of it. If you are not, he may well let you run around and do your own will until you can acknowledge that you are getting nowhere. Out of your sense of futility, you may be brought back to giving yourself to God.

Most people don't get personal notes from God on pivotal life decisions. If you are seeking God's will for a career, for example, you have some broad outlines to guide you. Since you will want to become a functioning part of a church, you will know that the church, not your career, is to be central to your life. That may eliminate some of the possible choices but will still leave open questions. If you can't see one of the choices above the other on this basis, perhaps you need to try to see if you are letting self-will skew your vision. This is a good place to invite others to speak into your life, if you haven't already done so. If there are still multiple alternatives it is probably because God has no preference in principle. God really does give his children freedom in the positive sense. He delights to see how we creatively live our lives to please him. What parent wants a robot for a child? What pleases a father is the child's free will turned in the direction of love and gratitude. For this reason, family refrigerators are covered with childish artwork and not with prints of professional artists.

There is, of course, a possibility that you might do better in one job than another, and it would be helpful if God would give you supernatural insight to see that in advance. God might well do that if his concern were your advancement in a job, but it usually isn't. God's concern is that you grow in loving unity with him and his church. He will protect you from well-intentioned decisions that would ultimately get in the way of that growth.

If you are not satisfied with this rather loose understanding of God's will, we may be back where we started. You can really count on God doing what he has promised to do—make you a saint—if you are willing for him to do it. You cannot count on him doing what he has not promised to do—make you successful according to an image of your own choosing. Much of our anxiety over God's will is actually anxiety about our own will. There is simply no reason to be anxious about whether or not God will lead us into his will if what we actually want is his will.

Fifteen

When Others Fall

But as for you, return to your God, hold fast to love and justice, and wait continually for your God.

Hosea 12:6

There remains one particular trap that I believe needs specific discussion. It is the tension serious Christians often experience between rigor and grace with regard to others. Whenever people come together for the purpose of pursuing holiness, this trap lies in wait. The pursuit of holiness requires a commitment to rigorous obedience to the will of God. Especially within a group that is dedicated to this there are always some people who, in the view of others, are falling short. If some people fall short, others will think they are betraying the ideal the group is striving for. If you perceive *yourself* as falling short, that is a different issue and one to be addressed through persevering in faith (see chapter 7). What I am now addressing is how to respond when we think someone else has turned away from the goal. At such times we will likely struggle with a tension between the desire to extend grace on the one hand and anger at his or her behavior on the other. This is a common and critical situation in the life of a church community, as well as an important divide in the road for the individual. At this juncture in the road, one way leads to holiness and the other into a ditch. The tension that arises when someone in a group of serious Christians seems to be straying from the path comes from a mind-set that places rigor and grace at odds with each other.

First, let's define the term "rigor." Rigorous simply means strict or unyielding. Put positively, rigor is an unyielding determination. In order to move toward holiness, a person must be rigorous—have an unyielding determination—to live in and for God. Holiness is strict undividedness toward God. So rigor, in that sense, is a quality of a saint. On the other hand, we can forget what we are called to and become rigorous—strict and unyielding—in regard to something else, and that makes holiness impossible.

When we don't have a good grasp on what holiness is and how to get there, we will be tempted to take one of two negative directions when we see others falling short: 1) ignoring the matter, or 2) being angry and/or self-righteous about it. In the first case, we might think we are extending grace, and in the second, we might think we are standing for a higher standard of holiness. The first option amounts to abandoning friends in need if they have in fact turned away from the path toward holiness. The second option is rigor turned in the wrong direction, which leads away from holiness. What we need is rigor turned toward the character of God. No other response is going to help people out of the ditch they have run themselves into. They need help to see they are in a ditch and help to see the way back to the road to holiness, but they cannot hear someone shouting from another ditch on the other side of the road.

Rigor and grace in perspective

The Apostle Paul was clear that everything depends on the grace of God toward us and that we must likewise extend it to others. He was also clear that this grace toward us was not a substitute for our rigorous dedication to doing the will of God. He called himself the Lord's bondservant because of the grace extended to him. Nevertheless, people around him had a hard time getting this in perspective. Some accused him of opening the door for sin, which would ruin the church. Others seemed to think that now that they were under grace they could go on sinning with no ill consequences.

Paul's ability to hold rigor and grace together doesn't come from his ability to perform a logical balancing act; rather, it comes out of his experience and understanding of God's response to sin. In chapter 2, I talked about Paul's understanding of the human condition. In Romans chapter 5 he speaks of a person being in Adam or in Christ. In the past, everyone was in Adam and inherited the curse that came from Adam's disobedience. Now, because of God's self-giving love, a person can be in Christ rather than in Adam. One can, in effect, be reborn and have a new representative ancestor through whom the blessing that comes from Christ's obedience is inherited. Obedience versus disobedience is the crucial turn. The absolute obedience of Jesus results in a blessing to all who are in him by faith. Paul goes on from there to talk about the human failure under the law and God's response to his people falling short.

> For just as by the one man's disobedience the many were made sinners, so by the one man's obedience the many will be made righteous. But law came in, with the result that the trespass multiplied; but where sin increased, grace abounded all the more, so that, just as sin exercised dominion in death, so grace might also exercise dominion through justification leading to eternal life through Jesus Christ our Lord. (Rom. 5:19–21)

God's law did not result in Israel having a thankful heart of obedience. The general response was not obedience but falling short, far short—rebellion. This is the universal witness of the Old Testament. If you read the Old Testament through from the beginning, by the time you get to the accounts of the destruction of Israel and Judah going into exile you should be thinking, "God would have been justified in giving up on them."[1] But that is not what Paul reports as God's response. He says, "Where sin increased, grace abounded all the more." *God's response to the sin of his people is grace.* This is a shocking statement. Modern Christians tend to overlook its implications. There is nothing, in Paul's words, that sets limits on how far God's grace will go. Grace seems to be open-ended. When sin increased, grace increased to outrun it. Period. This is how our heavenly Father, who is all love, has dealt with sin. *He is rigorous about grace rather than a set of rules.*

This is the essential perspective that holds rigorous obedience to God and grace together. The tension we feel in the matter arises from losing a handle on what God is concerned about and what we need to be rigorous about. The rigorous obedience God calls for is precisely love expressing itself in grace. "This is my commandment, that you love one another as I have loved you" (John 15:12). It is a fundamental misconception to think that judgment and anger on our part are signs that we are dedicated to doing the will of God. Yet people who set out to be serious about obeying God often fall into the trap of thinking that unlimited grace somehow undermines holiness.

The economy of grace is counterintuitive for human beings. We naturally assume that what Paul is saying about grace is leaving the door wide open for people to sin. Some people are *afraid* that such thinking is leaving the door open. Others are *hoping* he is leaving the door open. Very few naturally grasp the real implications. Paul addresses the distortion simply: "What then are we to say? Should we continue in sin in order that grace may abound? By no means! How can we who died to sin go on living in it?" (Rom. 6:1–2). And another example from earlier in his same letter: "And why not say (as some people slander us by saying that we say), 'Let us do evil so that good may come'? Their condemnation is deserved!" (Rom. 3:8). Paul's response to this charge is that it is ludicrous or worse. No one who grasps the awesome grace given to them can turn it around and use it as a license to go on sinning. Grace is a motivation to not sin, rather than a license to sin. If one thinks of grace as a legal arrangement, rigor will turn toward law enforcement on the one hand or self-indulgence on the other. If one has any idea of the blazing furnace of love who is our God and Father, rigor can only become unyielding determination to live in this love and to call everyone else to join in.

God's response to his people's shortcomings is that his grace increases to outstrip it. As the people of Israel increased in sin, God's grace went so far as to send his own Son, in human form, to deliver them from the hold that sin had on them. His grace extended beyond all limits because he is love without limits. As discussed in chapter 4, self-giving love is the fullest expression of God's character; it is the means by which he is transforming us into his likeness. How we respond to brothers and sisters who fall short and let us down will demonstrate how like him we are becoming. God's response to our brothers' and sisters' sin is that his grace increases. It is fueled by the unfathomable depths of his love. To the extent that we have come to live in and for him, our grace will increase too. It will be fueled from the same source.

Grace is not the passive way of tolerance. There is no love in mere tolerance. Tolerance is just the decision to preserve one's own peace by not being too annoyed. Grace is not looking the other way or telling me I'm on the road when I'm actually in a ditch. Grace is an act of self-giving love. It fiercely seeks to open a way for another to get back on the road to life and holiness. There is no specific program for the actions grace will take. We cannot say, "If someone does this, you should do that." Such instructions don't work. Our love is usually much too small to enable our grace to outrun another's sin when that sin affects us—especially when the other doesn't acknowledge the sin. Our love is too small to hear the voice of God through the wall of our own anger or our own self-centered interests.

God's love in us

Recognizing the real limitation, we must go back again to the basics. God is our loving Father. He is going to incorporate our lives into his own. I need to put this in personal terms, not in terms of principles. I have learned from Saint Thérèse to think of God as my loving Father and myself as a small child. (Being in my fifties is no limitation on seeing myself as a small child before God.) The rigorous obedience he wants from me isn't some kind of adult perfection; it is the presumptuous trust and dependence of a child. How I relate to my brother or sister who is falling short is not separate from the relationship I have with my Father. I learn to love my brother and sister by doing my childlike best to imitate my Father. As I do this, his love actually becomes mine.

> Father, I will give you a gift of love,
>   but I have no love that's mine to give.
> The love I know is what I see in you;
>   yet I will write my own name on it.
> I will pretend that I am rich in love.
> I will be your child and you will be my daddy
>   and we will play a game together,
>   a game of self-giving love.
> I will sit on your knee and pass out love
>   and you will give me more.

> I will pretend I am giving some to you
> and you will smile at me
> as though it were mine to give.
> I will give it out to everyone who passes by
> and you will be very happy
> because you will know
> it really has become mine to give.[2]

The more we respond to his love, the more he pours his love into us. We are enabled to love beyond just those who love us, for even sinners love those who love them. We will be able to love our enemies, and even our brothers and sisters who are letting us down. This is not just a theological proposition. His love changes me at an emotional and practical level. This is not an ability I can acquire as an independent quality of my own. I can only love with God's love while sitting in his lap. It is not something I can learn on my Father's lap and take away with me. I only have it while I am on his lap, but while I am there it is truly mine. Of course, if you are on God's lap, there's no need to get up and leave—ever. Oh distracted child, why do you not always remember that?

God himself is the source of the love that turns rigor into grace. In fact, the only rigor he wants from us is love. Jesus says this is the only purpose of all the obedience that God ever asked of his people. A man asked Jesus: "Teacher, which commandment in the law is the greatest?"

> [Jesus] said to him, "'You shall love the Lord your God with all your heart, and with all your soul, and with all your mind.' This is the greatest and first commandment. And a second is like it: 'You shall love your neighbor as yourself.' On these two commandments hang all the law and the prophets." (Matt. 22:36–40)

The corollary to this is that if you don't seek to love God and your brothers and sisters, there is no point in keeping the rest of the rules. Rigorous obedience has only one goal.

Taking the log out of my own eye

Sitting in God's lap doesn't get rid of the task of discerning what to do when others fall short. It simply makes discernment possible.

Often, when we discern clearly, we will see that the falling short we were so concerned about is not all that serious. Our anger or irritation was largely a function of our own self-centeredness. When another's action embarrasses or inconveniences us, our sin-detectors tend to go on maximum sensitivity. God's love often takes the log out of our own eye so we can see to take the speck out of our brother's (Matt. 7:5; Luke 6:42). When Jesus admonished the Jews about that, he was implying that the one who holds out for rigorous observance of the rules without grace was the one with the log, and the one who was breaking the rules had the speck. Love toward one another is what Jesus actually cares about. Keeping the rules is a small thing. If we intend to be rigorous about obedience to Jesus we must rigorously love one another. Such love is possible for us only within the Father's own love. From within the Father's love our inclination becomes to love as the Father loves and not to be rigorously inspecting for specks.

When people are running themselves into a ditch

There are occasionally serious sins that must be addressed. Sometimes people really turn from God's love and run themselves into a ditch. Living in the love of God does not make all the thorny problems go away. When believers really do get themselves in trouble, grace must not abandon them with platitudes about tolerance. Here we are faced again with the need for discernment. We must try to help them out of the ditch, but what should we use for leverage? If we yield to the natural temptation to use our own anger or self-righteousness, we will fall into the ditch ourselves. The only leverage that will have any chance of success is grace fueled by the Father's love. Unless we are anchored in our Father's love, we can do nothing helpful, and the temptation to deceive ourselves is very great.

Years ago I was Regional Director for the mission agency of an evangelical Protestant denomination. People often talked to me about problems within churches and within the denomination. These conversations were usually about someone else's misbehavior. They often started with the sentence: "I am concerned about (person's name)." I soon learned that "concern" was often a euphemism for: "I have a complaint about _____." Furthermore, the complaint was frequently being used as evidence to support the complainer's status as a guardian of the faith. The source of energy was not concern *for* the person under discussion. This is a common trap whenever we notice the shortcomings of others. It is a spiritual ditch we will surely fall into if we are not deeply rooted in the love of God. The first fruit of living truly in God's love is that we become concerned *for* people, rather than *about* them.

If we are concerned for a brother who has run himself into a ditch we will help him back on to the road. How we seek to help is crucial. What he needs is to renew his rigor at seeking God himself. He may well need to repent and start keeping some rules too, because holiness must take some form in the real world. However, the goal of living in and for God must not be obscured under a pile of behavioral demands. Rule keeping, in and of itself, has no power to give life, and we must not talk or act as if it does. In order to move toward holiness a person must be rigorous—have an unyielding determination—to live in and for God. Rigor must be applied to nothing else.

When I have failed at doing my part to help a brother or sister back onto the road to holiness, I have always been held back by my own failure of love. I have never failed for lack of an adequate pastoral strategy or practical knowledge of human behavior. I have simply let anger and frustration outrun grace. The only way I have ever found to avoid this is to seek God himself and to live in his love and allow it to grow in me.

No other counsel is necessary about rigor and grace than what we have established from the beginning: 1) Decide to want to become a saint. 2) Face the fact that you can't do it yourself. 3) Trust that God is going to do it in you. 4) Act accordingly. 5) Stick with it.

Our hope is in Jesus

This book has been written for one simple purpose: to help you continue on toward holiness. Holiness is not about self-perfection, it is about dependence—dependence on a loving Father who delights in his children, and has not only the power but the desire to make us into the saints he intended us to be.

And all of us, with unveiled faces, seeing the glory of the Lord as though reflected in a mirror, are being transformed into the same image from one degree of glory to another; for this comes from the Lord, the Spirit. (2 Cor. 3:18)

As it sinks in to our souls that this is God's will for us, let us respond with joyful abandonment of our own miserably limited life plans, and press on to know the Lord.

$\mathfrak{N}$OTES

Chapter 1: The Call to Become a Saint

1. See for example Romans 6:1–19. Note especially the words "present your members as slaves to righteousness for sanctification" (v. 19). Sanctification = holiness.

2. This passage is probably the clearest statement of this but it is by no means an isolated one. The formation of the church as the people of God is a major theme of the entire New Testament.

Chapter 2: An Undivided Heart

1. As quoted by Richard B. Hays in *The Moral Vision of the New Testament: Community, Cross, New Creation: A Contemporary Introduction to New Testament Ethics* (San Francisco: HarperSanFrancisco, 1996), 44.

Chapter 3: Humility

1. Nivard Kinsella, *Unprofitable Servants: Conferences on Humility* (Westminster, MD: Newman Press, 1960), 2–3.

2. Ernest Becker makes this case in *Denial of Death* (New York: Macmillan, 1975).

3. Hans Urs von Balthasar, *Two Sisters in the Spirit: Thérèse of Lisieux and Elizabeth of the Trinity* (San Francisco: Ignatius Press, 1992), 111.

4. Stephane-Joseph Piat, *Céline, Sister Genevieve of the Holy Face*, trans. Carmelite Sisters of the Eucharist of Colchester, CT (San Francisco: Ignatius Press, 1999), 164.

5. Piat, *Céline*, 151.

Chapter 4: Self-giving Love

1. *Elizabeth of the Trinity: Complete Works of Elizabeth of the Trinity*, vol. 2, *Letters from Carmel*, trans. Aune Englund Nash (Washington, DC: ICS Publications, 1995), 232.

2. Markus Barth, quoted by Hans Urs von Balthasar, *Theo-Drama: Theological Dramatic Theory*, vol. 2, *The Dramatis Personae: Man in God* (San Francisco: Ignatius Press, 1990), 155; from Barth's *Justification*.

3. In Old Testament Hebrew and in New Testament Greek, only one word is used for both righteousness and justice. Which of the two English words used is simply a translator's choice. In biblical language the concepts of righteousness and justice are the same thing. For our purposes here, it makes no difference which you choose.

4. Hans Urs von Balthasar, *Two Sisters in the Spirit: Thérèse of Lisieux and Elizabeth of the Trinity* (San Francisco: Ignatius Press, 1992), 328.

5. The expression "God who is all Love" comes from Elizabeth of the Trinity.

6. Christian dogma has always rejected "patripassianism," that is, the idea that God the Father suffered in the same sense as the Son. I am not arguing for such an idea. Christ is fully God, and the relation of his suffering to the experience of the Father and the Spirit remains within the mystery of the Trinity.

7. Richard B. Hays, *The Moral Vision of the New Testament: Community, Cross, New Creation: A Contemporary Introduction to New Testament Ethics* (San Francisco: HarperSanFrancisco, 1996), 197.

8. This story is central enough that all three Synoptic Gospels report it: Matt. 19:16–30; Mark 10:17–31; Luke 18:18–30.

9. Julian of Norwich, *The Revelation of Divine Love in Sixteen Showings* (Liguori, MO: Triumph Books, 1994, 1977).

Chapter 5: Faith

1. The language does occur in Psalm 20:4. Claiming this for one's desire for a swimming pool is of course completely out of context. It is worth noting that in Ezekiel 24:21 the language of "heart's desire" is also used as a prophecy of destruction.

2. Oscar Romero, sermon, December 25, 1977. See *The Violence of Love: The Pastoral Wisdom of Archbishop Oscar Romero*, comp. and trans. James R. Brockman, S. J. (San Francisco and Toronto: Harper & Row, 1988; repr. Farmington, PA: Plough, 1998), 40.

3. The most influential stream of this way of thinking comes through the Carmelites, stemming from St. John of the Cross and St. Teresa of Avila. St. Thérèse of Lisieux was also part of the Carmelite tradition.

4. *Letters*, vol. 1, 546. This reflects a Catholic view of suffering and one that we Protestants would do well to learn from.

5. A letter to her sister Céline, March 12, 1889, *Letters*, vol. 1, 546. Emphasis is Thérèse's.

6. To Céline, April 4, 1889, *Letters*, vol. 1, 553.

7. Brother Lawrence, *The Practice of the Presence of God* (Westwood, NJ: Revell, 1958), 53.

Chapter 6: The Obedience That Comes From Faith

1. The logic of this is further developed in chapter 10.

2. John 15:8–14 NIV: "This is to my Father's glory, that you bear much fruit, showing yourselves to be my disciples. As the Father has loved me, so have I loved you. Now remain in my love. If you obey my commands, you will remain in my love, just as I have obeyed my Father's commands and remain in his love. I have told you this so that my joy may be in you and that your joy may be complete. My command is this: Love each other as I have loved you. Greater love has no one than this, that he lay down his life for his friends. You are my friends if you do what I command."

Chapter 7: Perseverance

1. I have heard people argue that Jesus's prayers weren't always answered because he prayed in the garden that the cup of crucifixion would be taken from him. I see it as quite the opposite. It is the perfect picture of Jesus choosing his Father's will over his own, not of the Father denying Jesus's request.

2. N. T. Wright, *Jesus and the Victory of God* (Minneapolis: Fortress Press, 1996), chapter 10.

3. Ibid., 458.

4. I think the NRSV goes with "destined" rather than "predestined" simply because it is better English. Hanging "pre" in front of "destined" is really kind of redundant.

5. The above-quoted passage says he "chose us in Christ." It does not say, "He chose us to be in Christ." This is a statement about the blessing and assurance bestowed on those who are in Christ, not a comment on how one gets there.

Chapter 8: We and God

1. Cardinal Joseph Ratzinger, *Behold the Pierced One: An Approach to a Spiritual Christology* (San Francisco: Ignatius Press 1986), 27–28.

2. In the Old Testament we read of God making himself visible to the Hebrews in the desert as a cloud or fire, but that is something quite different from his literal embodiment in Jesus.

3. God resides in his church. Paul explicitly states it: "Do you not know that you [plural] are God's temple [singular] and that God's Spirit dwells in you?" (1 Cor. 3:16). The many people, the church, are the temple of God. God lives in the church.

4. The ways scripture talks about the relationship between Christ and the church involve the use of analogies: body, bride, temple, vine, etc. Analogies say something true about relationship while stopping short of literal meaning. It is relationship that we are concerned with, not speculation about the being of God as he is in himself.

5. There seems to be a confederacy of those who think of the cross as a symbol of nonviolent resistance aimed at getting the result they want. I think this misses the point, regardless of the nobility of the goal.

Chapter 9: The Role of Spiritual Disciplines

1. Hans Urs von Balthasar, *Two Sisters in the Spirit: Thérèse of Lisieux and Elizabeth of the Trinity* (San Francisco: Ignatius Press, 1992), 111.

Chapter 10: The Role of Scripture

1. This and other dates concerning Israel's history are taken from John Bright's *A History of Israel*, 2nd ed. (Philadelphia: Westminster Press, 1972).

2. See 2 Chron. 2:5–6 for a clear statement of the way the temple was understood.

3. Bright, 349.

4. Ibid., 372.

5. This has been mitigated a little by the current use of seminaries for ministerial training. Sometimes these become centers for the story of scripture to be placed in a pastoral context. For the most part, however, even seminaries that exist for pastoral training stick with the academic approach to the study of scripture.

6. Bright, 12.

7. It is historically inaccurate to see Greek thought as something that affected Christianity as distinct from Jewish thought. The Jews were affected by Greek culture, as were Christians. From the third century on, the Jews, even those living in Palestine, were surrounded by and immersed in Greek culture and thought. Some groups such as the Pharisees fought to avoid it. Others such as the Sadducees embraced it. On the whole, though, the Jewish views of scripture did not avoid it.

8. Bright, 20. Both traditions struggled to make sense of why this was a sacred book, and both understood it as in some sense a picture of God in relationship to his people. Origen was key to its popularity in later mysticism.

9. Bernard McGinn, *The Presence of God: A History of Western Christian Mysticism*, vol. 2, *The Growth of Mysticism: Gregory the Great through the Twelfth Century* (New York: Crossroad, 1994), 164–5. The sermons are contained in Bernard of Clairvaux's *Sermones super Cantica canticorum* (*Sermons on the Song of Songs)*.

10. Chester P. Michael and Marie C. Norrisey, *Prayer and Temperament: Different Prayer Forms for Different Personality Types* (Charlottesville, VA: Open Door, 1984), 31.

11. Ibid., 32.

12. Ibid.

Chapter 11: Mysticism

1. Thomas Merton, *Thoughts in Solitude* (New York: Farrar, Straus & Co., 1958).

2. Dylan Thomas, as quoted by Sally Leighton, "Going Gently Into That Good Night," in *Spiritual Life* (Spring 2000): 36ff.

3. G. K. Chesterton never wrote it in this form, but the substance of the idea is his.

4. Bernard McGinn, *The Presence of God: A History of Western Christian Mysticism*, vol. 2, *The Growth of Mysticism: Gregory the Great through the Twelfth Century* (New York: Crossroad, 1994), x.

5. It may also be described as Holy Spirit centered or Trinitarian. The point I am trying to make is that true mysticism recognizes God as the scripture portrays him.

6. Even spiritual teachers who claim to have discovered something profound all on their own have drawn their ideas from some spiritual tradition and end up teaching more or less in line with some established metaphysical tradition. In contemporary Western culture, this is often a version of Eastern religious pantheism combined with a bit of Neognosticism.

7. In this respect mystical experience is like any other spiritual gift. See 1 Cor. 12:7.

Chapter 12: Prayer

1. *The Way of a Pilgrim and The Pilgrim Continues His Way: A New Translation*, trans. by Helen Bacovcin (Garden City, NY: Image Books, 1978). The author is unknown.

2. This is what is called "the Jesus prayer" in Eastern Orthodox Christianity. Many in the West have adopted it as well. A slightly extended version is: "Lord Jesus Christ, Son of God, have mercy on me, a sinner."

3. John Cassian, *Conferences*, as published in *The Classics of Western Spirituality*, trans. Colm Luibheid (New York: Paulist Press, 1985), 132. He noted this formula as coming from Psalm 69:2, which in the numbering system of the English Bible would be 70:1.

4. Hans Urs von Balthasar, *Two Sisters in the Spirit: Thérèse of Lisieux and Elizabeth of the Trinity* (San Francisco: Ignatius Press, 1992), 438.

5. Jacques Ellul, *The Politics of God and the Politics of Man*, trans. Geoffrey W. Bromiley (Grand Rapids: Eerdmans, 1972), 190.

6. Letter from Thérèse to her sister Céline, August 15, 1892, *Letters*, vol. 2, 753.

7. While I reference my own experience in this matter, I think my view is also supported by Jesus's own life of prayer as discussed above. Our prayer arises out of conformity to Jesus in his prayer. It is not something we invent by ourselves.

Chapter 13: Possessions and Money

1. For a fuller perspective on this, see Hans Urs von Balthasar, *The Glory of the Lord: A Theological Aesthetics*, vol. 6, *Theology: The Old Covenant* (San Francisco: Ignatius Press, 1991), 316ff.

2. Richard B. Hays, *The Moral Vision of the New Testament: Community, Cross, New Creation: A Contemporary Introduction to New Testament Ethics* (San Francisco: HarperSanFrancisco, 1996), 125.

3. See ibid., 125n25.

4. Gerhard Lohfink, *Does God Need the Church? Toward a Theology of the People of God* (Collegeville, MN: Liturgical Press, 1999), 46–47.

Chapter 14: Discernment

1. Jeremiah 7:23 is an important example.

2. Hans Urs von Balthasar, *The Glory of the Lord: A Theological Aesthetics*, vol. 1, *Seeing the Form* (San Francisco: Ignatius Press, 1982), 46.

3. The ancient conception of mind (Greek—*nous*) includes much more than intellectual analysis. It includes judging, feeling, and perceiving. The point I am making here isn't to advocate rational analysis but our reasoning ability as a part of the process.

4. Hans Urs von Balthasar, *The Glory of the Lord: A Theological Aesthetics*, vol. 1, *Seeing the Form* (San Francisco: Ignatius Press, 1982), 241ff.

Chapter 15: When Others Fall

1. It is significant that this story is contained in the Hebrew scriptures themselves and is not the assessment of some outsider.

2. Note: This poem was originally written by Jack Bernard as a journal entry and also appeared on his memorial service bulletin.